Who Am I, Really?

Marie-Louise von Franz, Honorary Patron

**Studies in Jungian Psychology
by Jungian Analysts**

Daryl Sharp, General Editor

WHO AM I, REALLY?

Personality, Soul and Individuation

DARYL SHARP

For Rachel and the many years it took us to
understand what this book is about.

Canadian Cataloguing in Publication Data

Sharp, Daryl, 1936-
    Who am I, really?: personality, soul and individuation

(Studies in Jungian psychology by Jungian analysts; 67)

Includes bibliographical references and index.

ISBN 0-919123-68-6

1. Personality.   2. Soul.   3. Identity (Psychology).
4. Individuation (Psychology).
5. Jung, C.G. (Carl Gustav), 1875-1961.
I. Title.   II. Series.

BF698.S53 1995   155.2   C94-932027-7

INNER CITY BOOKS
Box 1271, Station Q, Toronto, Canada M4T 2P4
Telephone (416) 927-0355
FAX (416) 924-1814

Honorary Patron: Marie-Louise von Franz.
Publisher and General Editor: Daryl Sharp.
Senior Editor: Victoria B. Cowan.

INNER CITY BOOKS was founded in 1980 to promote the
understanding and practical application of the work of C.G. Jung.

Cover: Computer drawing by the author.

Illustrations by Vicki Cowan (except page 86 by J.K.
and page 104 by Joyce Young).

Index by the author

Printed and bound in Canada
by University of Toronto Press Incorporated

CONTENTS

See final page for descriptions of other Inner City Books

Jung in 1959, at the age of 84
(From Aniela Jaffé, ed., *C.G. Jung: Word and Image;*
photo by Hugo Charteris)

Personality is the supreme realization
of the innate idiosyncrasy of a living being.
—C.G. Jung, *The Development of Personality.*

Soul . . . is moving force, that is, life-force.
—C.G. Jung, *The Structure and Dynamics of the Psyche.*

Individuation is a process of differentiation, having for its
goal the development of the individual personality.
—C.G. Jung, *Psychological Types.*

The inner life finds few disciples among the hungry or the very well fed.
The hungry have their hands full scratching together enough to live;
the very well fed are too busy eating to pay attention.
Perhaps it is only those who have just enough who can
choose to be psychological.

—Adam Brillig, from an old notebook.

1
Manitoulin Matters

"There have been many in my life, both men and women, who did not like me. I don't wonder why. I was selfish, opinionated and mean spirited. I dare say I still am. Perhaps the only difference now is that I know it."

Professor Adam Brillig, inventor, explorer, retired Jungian analyst, Jack of some trades and one-time mountaineer of distinction, rested his paddle and turned his face to the east.

He was eighty-six years old and looked it. Deep wrinkles, wisps of silver hair, liver spots, watery eyes, thick glasses, all that and more. His almost bald pate was burnished brown, steel gray goatee neatly trimmed. His total height in elevator shoes was a shade over four-and-a-half feet. Standing, he could be a hobbit; stretched out, a lizard. To me he had a commanding presence in any position. I found it hard to think of him as anything but a wise old man.

"It's true," he said. "I was lustful too. I'd go after anything on two feet. And more than once I tried my luck with four."

Sunny, flopped loosely between the gunnels, looked up at him and thumped her bushy tail. She's big and looks like a wolf. The Humane Society thought she might be a cross between a Collie and a German Shepherd. I rubbed her ears and wondered why Adam was telling me this. He was a fairly recent addition to my small circle of friends and I had a perfectly workable projection on him. I wasn't keen to have it spoiled.

A light breeze sprang up and Adam secured the chin-strap on his Tilley, the kind of hat you see in magazines on people beside Land Rovers, alongside articles describing intrepid adventures in the Himalayas or the Sahara. Adam had been on such expeditions but never, to my knowledge, in a magazine.

"It has long been my habit," he continued, "to get to know a city from its underside. Perhaps *know* is an exaggeration. Better say I become comfortable. I prowl the pubs and observe. Sometimes I talk to people, and they to me, but on the whole I absorb the atmosphere in an introverted way. This would not be everyone's cup of tea, but what of it? It suits me just fine.

"Once in Copenhagen I spent an evening becoming acquainted with the local elephant beer. At 7.6% it packs quite a jolt. I watched a handsome young couple in their mid-twenties interact for an hour or so. She smiled a lot and never took her eyes off him. He was not so attentive. As they were leaving I touched the man's arm.

" 'Pardon me, do you understand English?' "

" 'A little, perhaps.' "

" 'Well, it is a long time since I saw such love in a woman's eyes. May I offer my congratulations?'

" '*Tak,* she knows not the language, I will say it to her.'

"I watched them leave, and when they got outside, why, didn't he give her a great whack that sent her flying into the street . . .

"You see, we hate what we are, we reject what we need. In frustration, we lash out at those we love. Behind all that, the very root of it all, is that we don't know how to deal with the opposites."

I could not gainsay this.

"I was not always so discerning," said Adam. "In my younger years I led a rather conventional, unseeing kind of life, which is to say I winged it, left hand knowing not what the right one did. The scales fell from my eyes when I went into analysis in Zürich. How I got there is a story in itself; well, you already know that circumstances led me to an impasse.[1]

"In Zürich I lived like a monk in two small rooms. I was used to being alone and I could speak the language, but still it was a difficult time. I had uprooted myself and had no close friends. I kept a journal of my thoughts and papered the walls with images from my dreams. I saw hardly anyone except my analyst, a kindly old man some

---

[1] See my *Chicken Little: The Inside Story (A Jungian Romance)*, especially chapters 3, 4 and 5. *The Compleat Brillig* is in preparation.

twenty years my senior. He was my life-line to the outside world. Once or twice a week I unburdened my soul to him. I would leave his office refreshed, a free man, though curiously he seemed to wilt. Only in retrospect, when I had my own practice, did I realize he was obliged to carry what I did not know about myself.

"My analyst was a man of few words and never gave direct advice, but after a time he wondered why I didn't get out more.

" 'Our time on earth is but a breath on the face of time,' he said. 'Think about your unlived life. Remember Ivan Ilyich?'

"Well, I didn't, but I soon found out. He was alluding to the short story by Tolstoy, 'The Death of Ivan Ilyich,' in which old Ilyich, a petty state functionary on his death-bed, laments his past. The poor fellow died in abject sorrow, with the painful realization that he had lived his life according to other people's values. For all his good intentions—or, and how difficult this was to admit, possibly even because of them—he himself had not lived at all.

"I took this story to heart and began haunting the area called the Niederdorf, the lower town, where bars and restaurants are open till all hours and ladies of the night stand on corners with umbrellas. At first I hung back; I just watched people and sketched them. Not bad likenesses, though I never fancied myself an artist; I did it just for the fun. Sometimes I attracted a small crowd. People from all walks of life—doctors and lawyers, secretaries, bankers, sewer workers, plumbers. Anyone with the wherewithal for a night on the town. They bought me drinks and we sang together, God love us!

"The Swiss have a dour reputation, but that's not my experience. True, they have an appetite for hard work, but they also know how to play. Especially when the wine-tasting ships are in, and at regular festival times, like *Fasching* in the spring and the fall solstice, Dionysus reigns. Then there are fireworks, dancing in the streets, costumes, balloons, music. I joined in and savored it all.

"Typically I'd stumble home, record the evening in my journal and put myself to bed. On occasion I'd be so fired up with drink and good feeling that I—or better say we, for by then my happy-go-lucky shadow had become an integral part of my life—would resolve to live on the street and give up the struggle to become conscious. Such decisions never survived a good night's sleep. But there were many times when I succumbed to an invitation to party, as they say, and once I ended up on the floor with a woman who bit my cheek. I still have the scar, see?

"My life since then has not been lacking in rich outer happenings, but I can still say, as Jung did, that I understand myself only in light of what goes on inside. Now I don't mean to imply that I'm in any way equal to Jung, or even the least bit like him. I'm much shorter, and although I've seen pictures of him with a mustache, as far as I know he never sported a beard."

It was an early morning in late spring, the second week of May. It was unseasonably warm for where we were, some 600 miles due north of Detroit and about 350 from my home in downtown Toronto.

Sunny and I and Adam Brillig were adrift in a yellow canoe in Lake Kagawong on Manitoulin Island, where there were only native Indians until about two hundred years ago. They still have rights to much of the land and their original place-names are very much alive. Manitoulin in Ojibway means "Spirit Island"; it is believed to be the home of the Great Spirit, Kitche Manitou. The word Kagawong means "where the mist rises from the water."

Manitoulin, the largest freshwater island in the world, is in Ontario at the top of Lake Huron. It is reached by car from Toronto in one of two ways. You can drive north to Sudbury for about four hours, west for an hour toward Winnipeg on the Trans-Canada Highway, then branch south at Espanola (pop. 6,000). Another thirty miles along a road sliced through the rainbow-colored Canadian Shield (granite and quartzite) brings you to Little Current (pop. 1,550), the northeast corner of the island, where if you're lucky you miss the fifteen-minute opening of the bridge, every hour on the hour, to let marine traffic through.

Or you can take the two-hour car ferry, the Chi-Cheemaun ("Big Canoe"), to South Baymouth from Tobermory, at the tip of the Bruce Peninsula, some 200 miles north of Toronto.

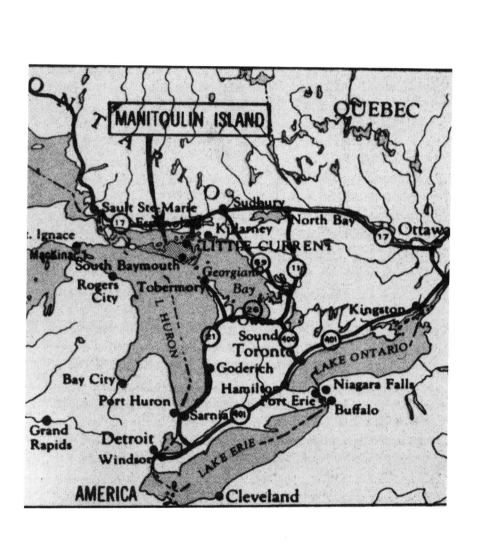

You can also fly to Manitoulin, via stopovers in Sudbury and Kirkland Lake. But that's expensive and they don't take dogs.

I had driven up with Sunny the long way in my little red Suzuki, a turbo hatchback. Seven hours, including a half-hour lunch break and two ten-minute rest-stops. After Little Current it was a scenic forty minutes to Adam's place. To our right we had glimpses of open water, the North Channel. To our left was dense forest on the side of rolling hills. Periodically there were those signs by the road that mean watch out for deer crossing.

The traffic was light and no one seemed in a rush. The road was well paved but not four-lane. There were farms and hamlets every few miles, but no billboards or shopping malls. The air smelled of sweet clover and fresh-laid manure.

I followed Adam's directions down a shaded dead-end lane to the edge of a lake. I opened the hatch and Sunny leaped out. She raced to the water and lapped up a gallon. Knee-deep she turned and looked at me, as if to say, "C'mon in, the water's fine." Projection? Perhaps the power to constellate. Else why did I tear my clothes off and jump in after her?

For a few minutes we splashed around. Sunny pretended to rescue me and I threw water at her. She snorted and paddled to shore. I rolled on my back and focused on the billowy clouds. I was sure I saw a face up there. I rubbed my eyes and it went away.

I waded back to the tiny beach while Sunny whipped around the yard, squatting at crucial points. Possibly she peed entirely at random; I couldn't prove otherwise. But the nature of our relationship persuades me that Sunny knows what she's doing even if I don't.

Adam Brillig, meanwhile, had appeared on the deck that ran along the front of the simple cedar-clad A-frame he called his home away from home. I waved and he helped me unload the car.

That evening we did not exchange much more than pleasantries. I was exhausted from the long drive and my mind was fuzzy. I napped on the couch while Adam rattled around in the galley kitchen. He called me to the table for a dish of Chinese glass noodles, stir-fried with bean-sprouts and virgin fiddleheads. Adam enthused about the local fauna and flora. He waxed eloquent on the spectacular sunsets and apologized profusely for the sudden torrential downpour that prevented us from enjoying one. By 9:30 Sunny and I were co-cooned under a cozy duvet on a cot in the loft.

I woke up in the middle of the night to the whirring of a bat, but that didn't bother me; they eat mosquitoes. Adam had a few bat houses in trees near the cottage.

"Gentle creatures of the night, they navigate by sonar," he said in the morning, "and occasionally one gets lost. Well, honestly, don't we all? Who among us can find our way in the dark, eh? Tell me that. I could plug the holes in the eaves, it's easily done, but I've never gotten around to it."

Now, three days later and just after 6 a.m., the mist was indeed rising, like a curtain in a theater only a lot slower. We could have been anywhere; I only knew we were afloat in a canoe.

Adam and I are both early risers. We'd been up at five and break-fasted on whole-wheat toast and porridge topped with brown sugar and fresh strawberries. That's way more than I usually eat so early. It took me back to below-zero Saskatchewan winters, when my mom would fortify me with Cream O' Wheat before sending me off to school with a Walt Disney lunch pail stuffed with Kraft cheese slices, meat loaf sandwiches and oatmeal cookies. Sometimes I would trade the cheese—for a boss marble, say, a multicolored aggie that would demolish all comers—but that's another story.

Adam had had his usual three-mile walk while I stared intently at the wall. I don't think these activities are all that different. I only prefer staring at the wall to walking because I find it easier to write, when something strikes me, if I'm sitting down. And out there you're at the mercy of the elements, a chill wind from the north or a sudden downpour, and you in a tee-shirt with no umbrella.

To tell the truth, I was glad to see Adam go. Since I'd arrived, his regular jaunts—he did the same again in mid-afternoon, just after a nap—were about the only times when I was entirely alone. Well, not counting Sunny. Of course Sunny does count, though not literally, having had no formal schooling that I know of. I can only say that when she raises a paw it more likely means she'll knock you down if you don't feed her, than four.

Anyway, although I'm inordinately fond of Adam Brillig, being with him is quite taxing. Like most acolytes, I suppose, I respect the master and hang on his every word. More, I crave his approval and would go to some lengths to get it. All the same I breathe a little easier without him.

Besides, I like being alone. Interesting things happen to me when I'm by myself. Or rather they happen *in* me; I just listen. Things also happen in me when I'm with other people, only I don't hear them so well because of the noise.

Hunched over my porridge, I watched the old duffer shrug himself into a windbreaker and plomp his Tilley on. He faced the mirror hung by the door and adjusted his hat to a jaunty angle. Then off he limped with his walking stick, a gnarled piece of elm with a carved crook ending in a beady-eyed snake head.

All in all, the past few days had been a restful time chez Brillig. We had not spoken a word on any serious subject. I busied myself making notes and browsing in Adam's bookshelf—pot-boilers for the most part, though tucked between *Angels in Heaven* by David M. Pierce and *Backgammon for Blood,* I found Rilke's *Letters to a Young Poet* and several volumes on local Ojibway-Chippewa legends—while he puttered around gathering kindling for the fireplace, reading cook-books and doing what-not.

I envied Adam, he never seemed at a loss. When the chores were done, he found something to read. If he didn't feel like reading, he sat. When he got tired of sitting, he'd walk about or simply stand, sometimes on his head.

Back home I thrive on work. When I run out of things to do I think up new projects. Nothing piles up on my desk. I meet every deadline well in advance, and never put off till today what I could do yesterday. It's very satisfying not to feel overwhelmed by things left undone. On the other hand, it takes a lot of energy to clear your desk every single day. And it's not possible either. There are always things that can't be finished. People you call are on holiday or no longer work there; they're on another line or you get their voice-mail; they're at lunch or only in the office Tuesday morning and Thursday afternoon between 1:30 and 3; they'll get back to you tomorrow. Or you get put on hold and that's the end of it.

Well, I do what I can and then I fret about the leftovers.

When I'm not working, my idea of bliss is to be in a warm place where I'm fed when hungry and no demands are made on me. Now there's a mother complex for you. This time at Adam's came very close to fitting the bill, as did the few cruise ships I've been on. Of course on a ship you can't get off any time. At Adam's you could step outside, if you had a mind to, and you were in the great outdoors. That was certainly a plus.

It had rained off and on. Rather more on than off, but when the sun was out I sat on the small sandy beach, and once I swam to little Bass Island about a thousand yards away. Sunny gave up half-way across and turned back. I soldiered on. The island was nothing special: a few broken-down shacks and a stand of evergreens. You could walk around it in five minutes. I side-stroked back, wondering what would happen if I drowned: what it would feel like, who would miss me, that sort of thing. Maybe I was feeling sorry for myself.

In the evening, after a light meal, Adam and I played gin rummy or Parcheesi—he had a whole cupboard full of games—while listening to a concert on the radio. We lit the old iron fireplace to take the chill off. On short wave we caught the six o'clock news from London; one night we listened to a play. Television was available on the island if you had a satellite dish. Adam said he had his hands full with radio. We could get a newspaper ten minutes away at Dave's Esso in Kagawong (pop. 210), but we didn't.

Clearly, Adam felt at home. I was trying.

Adam threw his arms out and stretched his little legs. The canoe swayed and Sunny whined.

"Will the sun come?" said Adam, eyes closed, palms open.

I did not answer. It was a morning ritual that I honored in silence. Adam's cottage was on the east side of the lake, facing west. The sun would soon come rising over the trees, if not hidden by clouds. Adam surely knew that, for he'd been coming here for years. But there he was, at the ready to offer his spittle, just as some African tribes used to, to make the sun feel welcome.

"Manitoulin matters," he said softly.

Yes, and I could see why. It was peaceful. No unwanted phone calls, no garbage trucks or meter readers, no door-to-door salesmen, no mail, no fax. There was lots of time to ponder. It was actually dark at night and in the fall, according to Adam, you could still see the legendary *aurora borealis,* the Northern Lights.

"It's a different world here," said Adam.

Yes, with black flies big as your fist and a cold floor in the morning, and don't forget to keep an eye on the plumbing. Try flushing down something more substantial than a turd and see what happens. That's the flip side of being in the country. You don't have to deal with such things in the Big City.

All right, I was mildly irked. In spite of the surroundings and my respect for Adam, I was bored. It isn't that I don't appreciate nature, it's just that it isn't enough. Even if I could tell one bird-call from another, or a trillium from a tulip, I'd still be restless. With considerable effort I had wrung some free time from my busy life. I appreciated the break and the lack of stress, but now I was anxious to get on with something productive.

"Adam," I said, "please, let's talk."

He knew what I meant. Since our collaboration in the launching of Chicken Little Enterprises, which continued to fare passing well, I had been at pains to create something new. Oh, I'd had a fair taste of public acclaim—interviews in journals, favorable reviews and so on[2]—but resting on laurels was not my way. Nor, I think, was I in-

---

[2] The media furor was both exhausting and invigorating. For awhile, collecting Ms. Little glyphs threatened to rival the trade in baseball cards. Personally I cringed at the exposure, particularly the talk shows, but my shadow loved it. Isn't that always the way? Or vice versa.

terested in garnering more. Pure and simple, I was driven by something inside. For sure I was in the grip of a complex, but which one and whether for good or bad eluded me.

What could I write next to promote an understanding of Jung's work? How might I reach more people? What new format could I devise? These were big questions for me. In search of answers I was always more or less distracted, not to say obsessed. I could forget it all while making love, but that's about it.

Adam indulged me.

"Porky Pig?" he suggested.

"Captain Marvel," I countered.

"Little Red Riding Hood."

"Johnny Appleseed."

"The Green Hornet."

"Abbot and Costello."

"Amos and Andy."

"The Little Match Girl."

"Rumpelstiltskin."

"Star Trek."

My mind buzzed with possibilities, but that was nothing new. Over the past few months I had fastened on a number of ideas for a day or two, but none had taken hold. Some friends urged me to invent a Jungian detective who solves mysteries from psychological clues. I gave it the old college try, but my heart wasn't in it. Maybe my life is mystery enough for me.

Come to think of it, what was *Chicken Little* if not a *roman à clef?* Who would ever have known that Ms. Little personified an archetypal motif, or of her close psychological link with the Sumerian goddess Inanna, if I hadn't cleverly assembled the evidence and then revealed it in a stunning finale, just like Agatha Christie's Miss Marples or a Hercule Poirot? It's true that I was as surprised as anyone, but I did write it.

I don't think of Jungian psychology as a religion, but I know I owe my life to it. Once upon a time I was on my knees. After a few years of analysis I could stand on two feet, more or less erect. That experience has colored my life. If someone were to ask, I'd be hard pressed to differentiate my single-minded zeal for Jung from the religious fervor that characterizes a born-again Christian, or any other evangelical for that matter. I'm not happy with this comparison, but there you are.

I poured coffee from the thermos and we drifted in silence. Now and then one of us would paddle a few strokes so we didn't stray too far from home. Where does my energy want to go? I wondered. That's really what I was here to find out.

Maybe I'd exhausted what I had to say about Jung. Maybe I should close my practice and sell the book business, quit writing too—do something completely different. I could learn Swahili or go into politics. I could go around the world, see new places, meet new people. I could open the lid on the Pandora's box of my unlived life. Wouldn't that be fun?

Sunny licked my toes. I fingered her long snout and stroked her noble head, hard enough to warm the fur like the books say to do if you want them to feel loved. She inched closer to get the message.

"Good dog, you're a very, very good dog."

Looking into her doleful eyes, I felt that whatever I did she'd be with me, every step of the way.

Yes, in a world of uncertainty I have Sunny. She follows me from room to room; she howls when I leave her alone and runs in circles when I return. I am her master and she turns belly up to show it. She woud brush my teeth if I taught her how. Sunny is true blue, a rare friend. And yet, at the same time, I suspect she'd go off with anyone who offered her a cookie. I don't know that for sure, but I wouldn't like to test it.

Such thoughts are a small measure of the opposites I've learned to live with, and one reason why I no longer give lectures. It used to be fun, saying my piece in front of a crowd. I was an authority; people looked to me for answers and I gave them. But one day I realized that whatever I said, the opposite was just as likely to be true. I was knocked off my perch by the ancient Riddle of the Cretan Liar, one of Adam's morality tales.

"Nothing I say is true," declared the Cretan Liar.

If that was so, then this statement too was a lie, which meant everything he said *was* true. Or did it mean he only told the truth when he lied? Perhaps he was lying only when he told the truth. What's the difference anyway? And who's to say?

Of course, writing books is problematic too, but at least you get to do it in private.

Adam expected his some-time assistant Norman to show up. Norman is a freelance professional photographer. He had been traipsing around Australia for the past two months, courtesy *National Geographic*, filming koala bears giving birth. Maybe he couldn't get into Mensa, but he's very good at what he does. His help was crucial in the unfolding Chicken Little drama, for without him we might never have thought of making a hologram of Adam's purloined Kraznac tablet, much less known how to do it.[3]

At my tentative suggestion Adam had also invited my two sidekicks, Arnold and Rachel.

"Though you mustn't count on it," he cautioned, "they do have their own lives."

Rachel and I have been close for fifteen years or so. We have a daughter but we aren't married and don't live together. She's rather more extraverted than I am, but we share an earthy appreciation for life. We have what I like to think of as intimacy with distance.

However, lately we had been more distant than intimate. After our holographic experiment in her basement Rachel had gone off with Adam to help with his research. Then she disappeared into her art.

We had spoken recently on the phone.

"Don't kvetch," she said. "I'll be back whenever. I'm working on something completely new."

I respected Rachel's passion for painting—quite as urgent as mine for Jung—but my world became smaller without her. Oh, I managed well enough. Nobody but me noticed that something was missing.

"Be patient," Adam counseled. "She'll either come back or not."

---

[3] See *Chicken Little,* chapter 8.

My friend and colleague Arnold was another matter. I was pretty sure he'd come because he was always around, more or less. Just when I think life is a bowl of cherries he throws me a lump of coal. We met in Zürich and lived together while we were training. We're more than close—brothers under the skin—though we're as different as chalk from cheese. I'm a Capricorn and he's a Leo, if that means anything. I'm scrawny and he's a bear of a man. And Arnold is a raving intuitive: he lives for what comes next. Myself, I'm mostly a sensation type; I walk on this earth. Unless I'm carried away by someone like Arnold, you can count on me.[4]

"My dear fellow," said Adam, "is all this not enough?"—sweeping an arm at the sky, the lake, the trees.

Well, I wished it were. This bald and gimpy octogenarian, this wrinkled dwarf with one foot in the grave, seemed genuinely content to wait for the sun; while I, hale and occasionally hearty, not yet sixty, was still trying to make it shine.

"Finding something to do is child's play," observed Adam. "The history of mankind is the history of what man has done—just for something to do. On the whole it is not a pretty picture. To my mind, the hero's task is finding out who you are when doing nothing."

The mist was almost gone now. Revealed to our audience of three were several fishermen in row boats patiently waiting for bites. The rising sun struck the tops of the pines on Bass Island. A family of ducks floated by, mamma and poppa and five little ones. Loons called from afar. It was very still.

It sure was beautiful. It reminded me of my teen-age years in Nova Scotia when the most exciting thing in life—well, next to the latest issue of *Amazing Stories* or a new sci-fi novel by Theodore Sturgeon—was going out fishing on a weekend for trout, hiking up and down mountain streams in rubber boots. My mom cleaned my

---

[4] These few words don't do justice to my long-standing association with Arnold, which is a recurring theme in my *Survival Papers: Anatomy of a Midlife Crisis* and *Dear Gladys: The Survival Papers, Book 2.* Arnold was also a partner in the Chicken Little business; in fact he was the one who enjoyed the talk shows.

meager catch of eight-inchers and we ate them. After supper I'd do my homework and then saunter over to the pool hall for a game or two with my buddies. It was a wonderful time; life was numinous.

Maybe Adam had some fishing gear stowed in his shed. He had told me about the salmon run on Manitoulin in the fall. Twenty-five-pounders wriggled upstream in shallow water to lay their eggs and then die. You could wade in and catch them with your bare hands. People came to watch from Michigan and Ohio and from as far away as Florida.

Maybe one day I'd have a go.

"Adam," I heard myself saying, "what do you make of the current interest in multiple personality disorder? They say it's a syndrome wide-spread among those who've been abused in early life. The traumatized ego splits into different parts in order to survive. Then in later life the split-off parts create havoc as different personalities."

"MPD," nodded Adam absently, fanning his paddle.

He fell silent.

I listened to the loons and watched the ducks. I thought about why I was here and what had happened so far: enough to get into the swing of things, maybe, but otherwise not much.

I listened and waited. And waited.

After awhile I began to wonder if this wasn't all happening in my head. I was alone in a canoe, talking to myself. Or was I? What if I were someone else? And not here at all? I longed for Rachel; she'd know. Sunny was with me, but all the same. I was close to panic.

"MPD," said Adam at last, "is demonstrably real."

I relaxed and bit into the peanut butter and banana sandwich I'd packed for a snack.

"The big question," said Adam, "is how to interpret it. To my mind it's just a new buzz word for what we've always called disso-ciation. If Jung's ideas were more widely known there would be no need to make such a big deal of it.

"Anyway, the MPD crowd don't have it quite right. The ego doesn't exactly split; although its characteristics may change, it's always an identifiable complex in its own right. What happens in response to a painful trauma is that the self-regulating function of the psyche gets activated and creates a complex that dis-remembers the event—it gets buried among the detritus of ongoing life. Like any other complex, it lies dogg-o in the unconscious until something triggers it. Then, wham!"

He dug vigorously into his paddle. For an old geezer Adam was remarkably fit. He was no Charles Atlas, but he had an air about him that would make a bully think twice before kicking sand in his face. I liked that; as an underweight kid with invisible muscles I had always felt so vulnerable.

I matched his stroke and we aimed for shore.

"The psyche is much like a pretzel," said Adam, "it twists in on itself. That's been suspected since Erasmus, and M.C. Escher made art of it. Jung gave it credence and mythology supports it. In time, *Deo concedente,* it will be generally accepted as a true fact."

At which he broke into song, in Latin if you please.

2
Who Am I, Really?

"Hmm, personality," said Adam. "Now maybe that's something we can get our teeth into."

It was early afternoon. We had lunched on macaroni and cheese, gussied up with bacon bits, shallots and diced green pepper. Adam was sipping crystal-clear lake water zapped by an ultraviolet jigger in the water line. I fingered a tumbler of Scotch, my second, stuffed with just enough ice to hold a swizzle stick perfectly erect.

We were lounging in the living room by a flickering fire, next to the picture window looking out on Lake Kagawong. Occasionally a fish broke the surface. The sun was shining and the trees sparkled, dripping wet after a violent but brief thunderstorm. Squirrels scurried from branch to branch, birds sang, flowers grew. Along the beach, some fifty feet away, a couple of mink trotted sedately by.

God or Manitou was in His heaven and all was for the best.

Adam filled and tamped his pipe. I rolled a cigarette.

"After some forty-odd years of being intimate with Jung," said Adam, "what others call psychology does not attract me at all. I read what's written and feel like throwing up. Psyche, remember, is Greek for soul, which to my mind is what psychology is all about. Carl Gustav Carus, Jung's namesake, knew that 150 years ago. What vision he had! In 1846 he defined psychology as the science of the soul's development from the unconscious to the conscious. Can you imagine how revolutionary that was? He recognized both the creative and compensatory functions of the unconscious, which Jung subsequently championed. But there's no soul in conventional psychology, which is to say the academic kind."

"You mean behavioral, experimental?"

"Yes," said Adam, "but cognitive and clinical too. In the main stream of psychological discourse, soul is *verboten*. Why? Because it can't be measured. Empiricism—that's modern science. Whatever you can't see, feel or touch does not exist. Clearly this approach to the world of things has been enormously fruitful; it is responsible for virtually everything we take for granted—machines, roads, houses, electricity, medicine, books and so on; in a word, civilization as we know it—but it has swept under the carpet many thousands of years' experience of the ineffable. Jung didn't berate scientists, he was one himself, but he did lament the loss of soul."

"Of course," I pointed out, "Jung was careful to distinguish soul in a psychological sense from its traditional theological meaning."

"Nor did he equate soul with psyche," nodded Adam. "He used the term psyche to include all psychic processes, conscious as well as unconscious. Soul he defined as personality, forged over time by an ongoing dialogue between the ego and the unconscious.

"That's just the point, you see. There's little recognition that soul is an integral element of personality. Developmentalists have by and large paid little attention to the discovery of the unconscious; at best, they give little weight to its influence. Developmental psychology as it is known today is only about building the ego. Not that I minimize the importance of a sturdy ego—dear me, no, we'd be lost without one—but that's far from all there is."

"Maybe it's just as well," I shrugged. "The unconscious is a can of worms. Conventionally trained therapists, without personal analysis, simply couldn't handle it. Perhaps they're better off ignoring the unconscious."

"That's as may be," said Adam, "but then a crucial element in understanding ourselves is left out. Of course, the academics acknowledge that we may grow to be a spruce or an oak, so to speak, according to inherited genes, but that's only common sense. So are the roles of the parents and the culture. But we aren't simply trees, thriving or not according to the soil. What has been forgotten, and what Jung confronts us with, is the part played by the unknown."

"Freud made a dent," I observed. If I'd put my mind to it I could have named a few others.

"So he did," agreed Adam. "But I was thinking especially of two things: first, the complexes and how they affect our lives; and second, the three levels of the psyche identified by Jung—consciousness, the personal unconscious, and the archetypal or collective unconscious, the objective psyche."

I wasn't sure where this was going, but I wasn't bored anymore. As a matter of fact my scalp was tingling, and in my experience that's usually a good sign.

"In conventional psychology," said Adam, "personality is understood strictly in extraverted terms—what we see of others, what we show of ourselves. Indeed, the American Psychological Association defines personality as an ingrained pattern of behavior that evolves as a style of life or way of being in adapting to our environment. Jung would call that persona.

"In the paper recently I read the reactions of friends to a boy's suicide. He was only seventeen. Everyone who knew him talked of a fine, upstanding young man with a sunny disposition and good potential. Several spoke of his 'wonderful personality'; an old girlfriend said he had 'personality *plus.*' His parents were bereft; they had thought he was happy. I don't disbelieve any of their comments, but we must assume, I think, that something was going on in him that wasn't seen by anyone, not his parents or his closest friends, something so painful that he felt it was all too much. What was happening behind his wonderful personality, which is to say his bright persona, that he couldn't live with? Besides the plus, there was apparently an unbearable minus.

"Unforeseen suicides are daily events, not to mention mild-mannered fellows shooting up restaurants or taking hostages, mates butchered and so on. In every case you hear of shocked family and neighbors. 'What a nice fellow he was,' they say, 'Who'd have thought it? She was always so helpful.'

"I think the bottom line here, psychologically, is that the general understanding of personality is too superficial. What you see is not all you get. What you see is persona. What's behind that—our shadow, things about ourselves we don't know or wouldn't show to others even if we did—is anybody's guess. Jung did his best to point that out, but to this day there are not many ears that hear."

I had found some carrot sticks in the fridge and I munched on these as Adam spoke.

"The dissociation of the personality," he declared, "is not confined to victims of abuse and it isn't pathological. I wouldn't be surprised if many of those diagnosed as having multiple personality disorders aren't simply neurotic. They're at the mercy of their complexes and don't know who they are, really. Analysis can fix that. Another batch are psychotic; they lack an ego strong enough to sort out the parts, and maybe they'll *never* know who they are. The rest are borderline, like us."

I thought of Arnold's oft-repeated remark that all analysts are crazy. "Except you and me"—his blue eyes gleaming—"and I'm not so sure about you."

"Mind you," said Adam, "I don't wonder that MPDers think they are on to something new, because under the right circumstances any complex can be activated. It erupts like a geyser and takes over. Then it functions as if it were the ego. So we find ourselves doing or saying things that in retrospect—when the ego's back in charge—we imagine are unlike us. 'Not I, but the devil in me,' that kind of thing. In many cases we have no memory of what happened and when confronted we make excuses. 'Sorry, I wasn't myself,' 'I lost it,' etcetera, etcetera. If it was something really bad we might claim to have been possessed by an evil spirit."

Adam rattled on. I half listened as in my head there appeared a vivid image of the so-called Azande Triangle, used by anthropologists to illustrate primitive psychology.

Among the Azande, a tribe in the Congo, it was customary to attribute sickness to either loss of soul or possession by a spirit. In either case the condition was believed to stem from harmful sorcery or witchcraft. That was one point on the triangle. The person who was ill, that is bewitched, went to the medicine man, the second point, for a diagnosis. The medicine man discovered the answer by means of an oracle—divination of some kind, like reading a toss of chicken bones or reflections in a bowl of water. That was the third point.

Then the medicine man directed his own powerful magic against point one, the witch or sorcerer. He might even have to travel to the underworld—through the Gateway of Clashing Clouds, say, or the Fiery Curtain of the Sun's Rays—to do battle with evil demons on behalf of his patient. All his efforts were directed toward recovering the lost soul or banishing the bad spirits.

That's not unlike what happens in modern therapy, though Jungian analysts, at least, don't favor an outside source. Bring it all home, we say, look in the mirror. We speak of possession by complexes, not spirits, and see loss of soul in depression, anxiety and hiding under the covers, symptomatic of the need to discover who we are. I suppose dreams are akin to an oracle, but our magic, if it can be called such, lies simply in facilitating an awareness of what's happening. When the soul rears its happy head, if it ever does, and the spirits dissipate, if they do, the patient hobbles off, "healed." Naturally we're pleased, but we don't deserve all that much credit. We are only midwives, and suffer alike when the new life we help to deliver is stillborn.

In another time and place, I believe Adam would be acknowledged as a medicine-man or shaman. *Mr. Second-Point Azande.* Yes, I like that; it has the ring of a quasi-truth. He has all the makings: sickly in early life, a keen intellect, unusual in appearance, a survivor of trials. Like the Greek god Hephaestus and the legendary Fisher King, guardian of the Grail, he limps. Well versed in the arcane, he has an unusual capacity for self-reflection. He is also a connoisseur of the evil men do; some of it he's done himself.

But of course for all his acumen Adam wasn't privy to what went on in my head. He was on his own roll.

"Magical thinking! Projection! Evil spirits! Most people are still psychological primitives, living in the Stone Age. Sure, we all revert to archaic attitudes in a crisis, but I'm talking about everyday life. We'd like to think we aren't responsible for what we do and how we feel. Stuff and nonsense! We're *always* us, and if a completely new side manifests, we might as well get to know it. Add it to the inventory of who we are.

"In short, we all have multiple personalities. There are those who think they don't, those who wish they didn't and those who have never thought about it."

Adam stopped and refilled his pipe.

"I'm rather glad I'm more than just a single me," I said, remembering how I used to feel guilty about being fragmented, not all of one piece. For a time there I feared I was schizophrenic: Dr. Jekyll one day, Mr. Hyde the next, and never the twain did meet. The mandalas I drew had pronounced fault-lines. My analyst wasn't worried though, he showed me some of his own.

"Make friends with your fragments," he suggested.

There are those who think analysis is bunk. I did too until I experienced it. Oh, I know analysis isn't a panacea and it doesn't work for everybody, but I got from it what I needed: confidence in my sanity and a theoretical structure to understand my moods.

"I name the others in me," I said now. "There's Gladys and Nicole, Billy-Joe and Bob's-Your-Uncle, Doolittle Dan, Flash the Fish and Picky Paul."

I could have added Adam Brillig   and Arnold and Norman; yes, and Rachel too—but I wasn't sure how Adam would take it. Or, indeed, if I believed it myself. I mean he seemed real enough to me, but so did all the others. Adam had a life of his own; they did too. And Sunny? Where was she in all this? I only knew I couldn't leave her out.

"There was a time when I felt lonely," I said. "Now I never do."

"Those others want a voice too," said Adam, "and if the ego

doesn't grant it willingly, they'll take it. Oh, you know what I mean. Complexes are autonomous, just as if they were other people. They disturb our memory and interfere with our will; they come and go according to their own laws; they obsess consciousness and influence our speech and actions. They are saints; they are sinners. They can't be destroyed, but with insight their energy can be harnessed."

He filled his glass from the tap and held it up. "To death, taxes and the rising sun," he toasted, "add another sure thing: if you aren't conscious of your complexes you'll be pole-axed by them."

"I'll drink to that," I said, doing so.

Adam went to the window. I opened a can of cashews.

"Jung calls complexes gods," I noted.

"And why not?" replied Adam. "That's what they've traditionally been known as. Lacking our modern knowledge of the psyche, complexes have always been personified as gods. Of course now we'd call that projection—which is simply a natural inclination to see in the outside world unacknowledged aspects of ourselves—but the pantheons of past cultures are of inestimable metaphoric value.

"Look around. Do we not see in the woman who would sacrifice relationship for career an echo of the Greek goddess Athena, that iron-willed father's daughter who sprang fully-grown, with a mighty shout, from Zeus's head? Is not a father who constrains his offspring from following their individual path analogous to the malefic Saturn who gobbled up his children? Are not those who break free of the parental complexes akin to heroes, dragon-slayers like Perseus? Don't those who shed light on their own psychology owe a debt of gratitude to the crafty Prometheus who stole fire from the gods? Did not Dionysus personify an archetypal pattern of indestructible life?"

My mind was awhirl.

"Clap hands!" cried Adam, doing a cartwheel that took him dangerously close to the fire. "The psyche thrives on metaphor. It lives and breathes the symbolic. Do not alchemical treatises spell out the process of turning a leaden you into gold? When you understand the historical evidence and grasp what is at stake on a personal level, why then individuation begins!"

Sunny barked and scrambled to her feet. She loped to the screen door and banged her head against it. She's over seventy in human years. Her eyes are failing but there's nothing wrong with her nose. Just outside on the deck there was the cutest little chipmunk nestled in Sunny's bowl, eating her left-over breakfast.

I let her out to reclaim her turf and turned to Adam.

"I am used to thinking of gods as complexes, or vice versa, but few people are, including many who practice therapy."

"Well it's their loss," harrumphed Adam. "Give them a decent education in the humanities and they'll smarten up. Mythology, literature, theater, the fine arts, it's all there. That's one of the basic problems with Western culture pinpointed by Jung. Our education system is oriented to the child, but who is to educate the educator? What of the child, the primitive, within the grown-up?"

He limped over to rummage in a trunk in the corner. Even with my inferior intuition I had a good idea what he was after. Adam is the only person I know, besides myself, who travels with a complete set of Jung's Collected Works. He pulled out a book and leafed through it. "Listen to this," he said:

> Our age has been extravagantly praised as the "century of the child." This boundless expansion of the kindergarten amounts to complete forgetfulness of the problems of adult education . . . . Nobody will deny or underestimate the importance of childhood; the severe and often life-long injuries caused by stupid upbringing at home or in school are too obvious, and the need for more reasonable pedagogic methods is far too urgent. But if this evil is to be attacked at the root, one must in all seriousness face the question of how such idiotic and bigoted methods of education ever came to be employed, and still are employed. Obviously, for the sole reason that there are half-baked educators who are not human beings at all, but walking personifications of method. Anyone who wants to educate must himself be educated. But the parrot-like book-learning and mechanical use of methods that is still practised today is no education either for the child or for educator.[5]

---

[5] "The Development of Personality," *The Development of Personality,* CW 17, par. 284. [CW refers throughout to C.G. Jung, *The Collected Works*]

"Sounds to me like the beginning of a rant." I said.

Of course I was quite familiar with Jung's essay; I had once done a paper on it. I was just egging Adam on, to see how far he'd go.

He paced the room. It wasn't all that big. About twenty-five feet long; and in width, if he and I and Sunny lay head to toe, we'd be brushing the walls.

"Our education system," said Adam, "suffers from a one-sided approach to the child who is to be educated, and from an equally one-sided lack of emphasis on the character of the educator. People like to speak of training the child's personality. But what of those doing the training? What about their personalities? Parents for the most part are incompetent. As often as not they're half children themselves and will always remain so. This is no secret; it's so well known that we expect great things of trained professionals, heaven help us, self-styled experts stuffed full of soulless psychology and ill-assorted views on what constitutes personality.

"I dare say you've seen them, posturing in halls of learning, pontificating in print and on TV—shallow-pates, inflated peacocks more interested in showing off what they know than in caring for the young. They are solidly convinced of their competence and feel grown up. They are no more nor less than what you see, living proof that people really do exist who believe they're what they pretend to be. Woe betide if they were ever to doubt themselves; uncertainty would cripple them, undermine their authority. The truth, by and large, is that they suffer from the same defective education as their hapless young charges, and have just as little personality. "

Adam read:

> The fact is that the high ideal of educating the personality is not for children: for what is usually meant by personality—a well-rounded psychic whole that is capable of resistance and abounding in energy—is an *adult* ideal. It is only in an age like ours, when the individual is unconscious of the problems of adult life, or—what is worse—when he consciously shirks them, that people could wish to foist this ideal on to childhood.[6]

---

[6] Ibid., par. 286.

"Imagine!" said Adam. "Jung wrote that more than sixty years ago and hardly anything has changed. We still talk about educating the literal child—the best system, the right approach, which method will get the best results and so on—when our real concern should be with the child in the adult!"

He was in full flight now. Head tucked into his shoulders, he prowled about like a restless armadillo.

"In each of us there lurks a child, an eternal child, something that is always becoming, never completed, requiring unceasing care, attention and education. That's the part of the personality that wants to develop and become whole. Who among us has given it full rein? Who has even tried? Dimly suspecting our own deficiencies, we seize upon child education and fervently devote ourselves to child psychology, fondly supposing that what went wrong in our own upbringing can be corrected in the next generation. The intention is commendable enough, but it founders on the psychological fact that we can't correct in our children the faults and mistakes we ourselves are still unconscious of."

Sunny scratched at the door and I let her back in.

"I think kids aren't half as stupid as we imagine," I offered. "They know very well what is genuine and what isn't. They have an innate sense of what's right and what's wrong."

Why just the other day my twelve-year-old daughter Jessy Kate, whose favorite cousin is a gay entertainer in show-biz, told me that homophobia sucks. I don't think she got that from her teachers.

"Yes," agreed Adam. "And so they rightly resist being bamboozled by their so-called betters. It's an interesting variation on the old saw about the Emperor with no clothes. Educators don't lack the right clothes—which is to say they present a spiffy persona—but often there's no one in them."

The afternoon sun was beaming in, revealing cobwebs in every corner. Here a mote, there a mote, everywhere a dust-mote. Adam did for himself quite well, considering, but clearly he could use a good cleaning lady, or man (though I didn't think there'd be many males on Manitoulin who did that kind of work).

Actually, about the only surprise for me in what Adam was saying was that he still cared. As he stoked the fire into a blaze I wondered: if I ever get to be his age, wouldn't I rather be hanging out on a beach with Rachel than prodding a log? But what if I were the log? Now there's food for thought.

"The persona," said Adam, "is simply that which in reality one is not, but which oneself and others are tempted to think one is. Jung calls it a functional complex that comes into existence for reasons of adaptation or personal convenience. Fundamentally it is nothing real; it is a compromise between individual and society as to what we should appear to be. We take a name, earn a title, exercise a function; we are this or that. You, for instance, are analyst, publisher, writer, father, but such labels say little about who you are, really.

"In a certain sense our personas are real, yet in relation to the essential individuality of a person, one's personality, they are only a secondary reality, a compromise formation in the making of which others often have the greater share. In a word, the persona is a semblance, a two-dimensional reality without depth."

He paused for breath.

"We couldn't do without one though, eh?" I put in.

"Indeed not," agreed Adam. "Those who lack a decent persona are a sorry lot. They slip from one social gaffe to the next, narcissistic bores or appealing children, always taking forgiveness for granted; blind to the world, hopeless dreamers, innocents abroad.

"Of course it's one thing to have a well-developed persona and to be conscious of it—knowing that the hat you wear, the face you show, is a temporary act—and quite another to be identified with it. That's where most of us come unstrung. We don't know who we are outside our roles. We have persona but no personality."

I believed this, but I knew too that I couldn't always tell the difference. I admitted as much to Adam.

"I tend to take people at face value."

"You are easily taken in, my friend."

It was true. In analytic sessions, where I am paid to be psychologically perceptive, that kind of energy is constellated; sometimes I can see around corners and even understand dreams. But out in the world I'm a patsy. I seldom question what looks good. I respond with favor to an open smile and a firm handshake. I have a drawer full of magic beans and only flatulence to show for it.

"Personality comes from the guts," declared Adam. "The persona, however, is more or less identical with a typical attitude, dominated by a single psychological function, be it thinking, feeling, intuition or sensation. This one-sidedness necessarily results in the relative repression of the other functions. In consequence, the persona is a decided obstacle to the individual's psychological development, and its dissolution is an indispensable condition for individuation.

"Likewise, it is not possible to individuate by conscious intention, because that invariably is led by the typical attitude, which excludes whatever doesn't fit in with it. What is required, rather, is the assimilation of unconscious contents, a process in which conscious intention takes a back seat and is supplanted by what on the face of it seems irrational. This process alone signifies individuation, and its product is individuality: particular and universal at once."

These words were not new to me, but coming from Adam they fairly glowed; indeed, they became brilligant.[7]

"I would like to think you youngsters know what's at stake," he said, moving slowly toward the stairs.

I glanced at my watch: nap-time. Adam was winding down.

"The world will go to pot if we let it, and I don't mean marijuana. We're on the brink of the Great Disaster, the apocalyptic end of everything. The catastrophes confronting us today are not elemental happenings of a physical or biological order, but psychic events. In every quarter of the globe we are threatened by wars and revolutions that are nothing other than psychic epidemics. At any moment mil-

---

[7] I am indebted to Håkan Raihl, director of the Center for Jungian Psychology in Stockholm, for this adjective to describe the impact of Jung's views when mediated by Adam. I believe that in time it will find its way into the Oxford English Dictionary *("brilligance,* n., the ability to illuminate the ideas of another; hence *brilligant,* adj."), thereby immortalizing Adam Brillig, just as *mesmerize* recalls the Austrian physician Franz Anton Mesmer (1734-1815), who cured his patients by enthralling them.

lions of human beings may be smitten with a new madness, and then we shall have another world war or devastating civil conflict.

"Once we were at the mercy of wild beasts, earthquakes, landslides and so on. Now we are battered by the elemental forces of our own psyche. This is the World Power that vastly exceeds all other powers on earth. The Age of Enlightenment, which stripped nature and human institutions of gods, overlooked the God of Terror who dwells in the human soul.

"Greeners talk about getting our act together globally and what will happen if we don't. Their hearts are in the right place, but I'm afraid they're barking up the wrong tree. Conservation? Environmental control? Holes in the ozone layer? All that's important, of course, but just a piss in the ocean compared to being unconscious."

Adam supported himself on the banister.

"The world teems with people who know a lot," he said, "but let us not confuse the Faustian accumulation of knowledge with being conscious, much less individuation."

He pulled himself up the steps and left me staring at the wall.

I was still making notes when Adam reappeared about five.

"There's nothing like a stint with Orpheus to put lead in your pencil," he said, rubbing his hands briskly.

He took his coat and Tilley off the peg and prepared himself for his usual outing.

"Adam," I said, "would you mind taking Sunny? I think she'd like a W-A-L-K."

I spelled it out because it's a complex trigger for Sunny. When she hears the word "walk" she's up and running. I don't begrudge her the exercise, but if you don't happen to feel like it she might tear your throat out. At least that's my fantasy.

"Not at all," smiled Adam. "Thought you'd never ask."

And off they went, one with a limp and one with a lope, one with gout and one with a snout; he not much taller than she.

3

Personality Plus

Alone, I delved into my suitcase and found volume 7 of Jung's Collected Works: *Two Essays on Analytical Psychology.* I think it's the best introduction to the broad scope of his ideas. In one or other of these essays—"On the Psychology of the Unconscious" and "The Relations Between the Ego and the Unconscious"—Jung touches on all his basic concepts: typology, complexes, persona, shadow, anima/animus, projection and individuation. It also becomes clear why he broke with Freud.

I always find something new, or nuggets I've forgotten, in *Two Essays.* As now, for instance, I read:

> Human beings have one faculty which, though it is of the greatest utility for collective purposes, is most pernicious for individuation, and that is the faculty of imitation. Collective psychology cannot dispense with imitation, for without it all mass organizations, the State and the social order, are impossible. Society is organized, indeed, less by law than by the propensity to imitation, implying equally suggestibility, suggestion, and mental contagion. But we see every day how people use, or rather abuse, the mechanism of imitation for the purpose of personal differentiation: they are content to ape some eminent personality, some striking characteristic or mode of behaviour, thereby achieving an outward distinction from the circle in which they move. We could almost say that as a punishment for this the uniformity of their minds with those of their neighbours, already real enough, is intensified into an unconscious, compulsive bondage to the environment. As a rule these specious attempts at individual differentiation stiffen into a pose, and the imitator remains at the same level as he always was, only several degrees more sterile than before. To find out what is truly individual in ourselves, profound reflection is needed; and suddenly we realize how uncommonly difficult the discovery of individuality is.[8]

---

[8] "The Relations Between the Ego and the Unconscious," CW 7, par. 242.

Now there's a screed if I ever read one. Jung was adept at haranguing his readers when writing about something he passionately believed in. Take the following:

It is a notorious fact that the morality of society as a whole is in inverse ratio to its size; for the greater the aggregation of individuals, the more the individual factors are blotted out, and with them morality, which rests entirely on the moral sense of the individual and the freedom necessary for this. Hence every man is, in a certain sense, unconsciously a worse man when he is in society than when acting alone; for he is carried by society and to that extent relieved of his individual responsibility. Any large company composed of wholly admirable persons has the morality and intelligence of an unwieldy, stupid, and violent animal. The bigger the organization, the more unavoidable is its immorality and blind stupidity. . . . Society, by automatically stressing all the collective qualities in its individual representatives, puts a premium on mediocrity, on everything that settles down to vegetate in an easy, irresponsible way. Individuality will inevitably be driven to the wall. . . . Our admiration for great organizations dwindles when once we become aware of the other side of the wonder: the tremendous piling up and accentuation of all that is primitive in man, and the unavoidable destruction of his individuality in the interests of the monstrosity that every great organization in fact is. The man of today, who resembles more or less the collective ideal, has made his heart into a den of murderers, as can easily be proved by the analysis of his unconscious, even though he himself is not in the least disturbed by it.[9]

Pretty strong stuff. If you had a key to a corporate washroom and read that, it might make you cringe. Or at least wince. Of course it's pretty unlikely you'd ever read it; you'd have far more important things to do. And even if you did, and it hit home, more likely you'd go to the Bahamas for a week than get serious about who you were. As a matter of fact I've been there, though not to the Bahamas. I escaped with my soul before I knew I even had one. To be honest, I would have to say that was more luck than wit. I *liked* working for Procter & Gamble and never thought of it as a monstrosity. The pay

---

[9] Ibid., par. 240.

was good and I had lots of responsibility. I didn't feel immoral or stupid. I only left because I was nagged by the possibility of something else, as if I'd been spooked by Arnold before I even met him.

Well, that was a long time ago. Now I hardly ever think about my past unless I'm reading Jung. There's no more life in those days for me than the faded photographs you find in a drawer when looking for something else.

I poked around and put together a snack: soda crackers and Ritz biscuits, old Canadian cheddar, Atlantic oysters and black olives, a small jar of Swedish caviar (well, lumpfish) and celery sticks.

Adam and Sunny banged through the door as I was setting this out. Sunny went immediately to the toilet and pried the lid up to get a drink. Adam eyed the plate.

"Good fellow," he smiled.

Humming to himself he poured a shot of water.

"Like some?"

"A knuckle of Scotch, thanks. Choke it with ice."

Adam always came back from a walk in high spirits. Maybe it was the clear Manitoulin air, the heady mix of flowers in bloom and fertilizer. Or maybe he had a lady friend down the lane. I wouldn't say he's past it.

"Now where were we," he said, munching a Ritz sandwich.

He was at the window, gazing at the lake. For a second or two he resembled my father. This was disconcerting to me, since they have almost nothing in common. My father has just as little hair, but he's almost two feet taller and not quite as old. Before he retired he was an accountant and he's never had the slightest interest in psychology.

I blinked at my notes.

"Child education . . . personality . . ."

Adam did an abrupt turn. It was as if his blood began to race and he had to keep up with it.

"Yes, well, I can't tell you how many parents used to come to me with the intention of sparing their children the unhappy experiences they went through in their own childhood. As if they could save them from the trials of life. And when I asked, 'Are you sure you've got yourself in order?' they'd nod brightly, 'Oh, quite sure.'

"It wasn't true, of course. If they were brought up too strictly, they spoiled their own children with a tolerance bordering on bad taste. If certain matters had been painfully concealed from them in childhood, they went to the other extreme and revealed them with a lack of reticence that was just as painful. If there's something we'd like to change in our children, you see, we are well advised to first consider whether it might better be changed in ourselves.

"In many respects we are all children. Personality is a seed; it develops by slow stages throughout life. There is no personality without definiteness, wholeness, ripeness. Such qualities cannot and should not be expected of a child, for what then would happen to childhood? We don't need more pseudo-grownups. Modern education has given birth to enough such monstrosities: children goaded on to make up for their parents' most dismal failures, burdened with ambitions that can never be fulfilled.

"Think of those who set themselves the fanatical task of doing their best for their children, living only for them. This ideal effectively prevents the parents from doing anything about their own development. Knowing nothing about projection, they thrust their best down their children's throats, which often means what they've neglected in themselves, the potential they haven't lived."

Volume 17 of Jung's Collected Works was still on the table. Adam picked it up and found this passage:

What usually has the strongest psychic effect on the child is the life which the parents (and ancestors too, for we are dealing here with the age-old psychological phenomenon of original sin) have not lived. This statement would be rather too perfunctory and superficial if we did not add by way of qualification: that part of their lives which *might have been* lived had not certain somewhat threadbare excuses prevented the parents from doing so. To put it bluntly, it is that part of life which they have always shirked . . . . [that] sows the most virulent germs.[10]

[10] "Introduction to Wickes's 'Analyse der Kinderseele' *[The Inner World of Childhood],* " *The Development of Personality,* CW 17, par. 87.

"That's the sorry picture," declared Adam. "What we don't know about ourselves, the next generation will pay for. Unwittingly, intent on doing our best, we are just as likely to pass on our worst—our unacknowledged shadow. This has long been known. It's an archetypal pattern documented in Greek mythology as the curse of the House of Atreus."

The House of Atreus! Jeez, Adam had a gift for nutshells.

Just then Sunny jumped up barking and raced to the door. She always does that when someone's coming. Noise hurts my ears and I've thought of trying to train her out of it. So far though, I'd rather have the warning.

I looked out the kitchen window to see Rachel rolling up in her white station wagon. Beside her was our daughter Jessy Kate. In the back seat were Arnold and Norman.

Sunny and I were out the door in a flash.

"We took the ferry from Tobermory; it wasn't half bad," said Norman, unwinding his long legs and stretching.

"Where am I?" coughed Arnold, rubbing his eyes. He staggered around like he was demented. Arnold had once been a celebrated actor and from time to time he still played the fool.

Adam was amused.

"Welcome!" he said.

I was already wrapped around Rachel. Glad to see her? I'll say. Sunny too, she leaped and yapped and rolled in the grass. Then I hugged J.K., as Jessy likes to be called—"Why, you're taller than your mom!"—and we took their bags inside.

That evening Adam made potato and onion pancakes—*latkes,* like my Russian Gramma used to make, and almost as good—brushed with olive oil and topped with sour cream, a light Caesar salad on the side. Rachel had brought a home-made Black Forest cottage cheesecake and a selection of fruit from a roadside market. Norman produced a box of chocolate mints; Arnold came up with a vintage bottle of Clos-de-Vougeot, a rich French Burgundy from a small vineyard south of Dijon.

It was like a college reunion, an Old Home Week. I've not actually been to one but I have an active imagination. We knew each other well enough to feel comfortable and we could say pretty much what was on our minds. Also, except for J.K., as joint stockholders of Chicken Little Enterprises we all had a vested interest in what happened next.

After supper Adam and I brought the others up to date.

"I don't say it will set the world on fire," I finished, "but I think it has possibilities."

"Here, here," clapped Arnold.

That was predictable. Arnold likes the open ended; structure makes him claustrophobic. He'd had a field day designing Ms. Little glyphs for tee-shirts and up-market lingerie. We didn't use them because they were too lewd. I've learned a lot from Arnold about what's possible, but not much about what's workable.

"Well," said Rachel, looking dubious, "Jung does redefine the concept of personality, don't you think? I mean he doesn't use it the way it's generally understood."

"Yes," conceded Adam, "but rather than redefine, I'd say he encourages a deeper understanding of what's involved, a perspective more in accord with general experience—the *consensus gentium,* as Jung would say, what has always and everywhere been believed."

"To be fair," said Norman, "and with all due respect to the consensus whatever, there are many opinions on what constitutes personality. It's hard to know what to believe."

"What's to believe?" asked Adam. "Only experience. Outside of personal experience we're at the mercy of so-called experts. There are those who think their opinions give them a solid base, but that's all in the head. Opinions, often as not, come from complexes; like the pronouncements of experts, they may have little to do with truth."

And then, to my surprise, for I thought he must have had enough for one day, Adam launched into an oration.

"Personality can only be mentored by someone who has it. And one can only achieve personality as the fruit of a full life: activity coupled with introspection, confidence tempered by a healthy dose of self-doubt. The achievement of personality means nothing less than the optimum development of the individual human being. It is impossible to foresee the endless variety of conditions that have to be fulfilled. A whole lifetime, including all its biological, social and spiritual aspects, is needed.

"According to one of Jung's several definitions, personality is the supreme realization of the innate idiosyncrasy of a living being. On the one hand it is an act of high courage flung in the face of life, the absolute affirmation of who one is. On the other hand it involves accepting some universal conditions of existence, such as where we find ourselves on this earth and having a physical body. To educate our young to the necessity and intrinsic value of undertaking this lifelong journey is surely the hardest task we can set ourselves."

I stole a look at Rachel. She was evidently enjoying this. More, as in our original encounter with Adam, she was enthralled.[11] That's a father complex for you. I don't mean to say she's not discriminating. Rachel wouldn't sit at the feet of any old man. She's not easily seduced and she has good taste.

J.K., I noticed, was minding her own business, making bead pouches and facsimiles of native dream-catchers. Samples of her work had been passed around the dinner table and pronounced excellent. She had sold some to her classmates and local stores; she knew about mark-up and discounts and what her time was worth. Practical math; like receding hair, it runs in the family.

"Personality," Adam was saying, "develops in the course of life from germs that are almost impossible to discern. It is only our deeds that reveal who we are. We are like the sun, which nourishes the life of the earth and brings forth every kind of strange, wonderful and evil thing; we are like the mothers who bear in their wombs, *in potentia,* untold happiness and incomparable suffering. Just as the sun shines upon the just and the unjust, and as women who bear and give suck tend God's children and the devil's brood with equal compassion, unconcerned about the possible consequences, so we also

---

[11] See *Chicken Little,* chap. 5.

are part and parcel of this amazing nature and, like it, carry within us the seeds of the unpredictable. At first we do not know what deeds or misdeeds, what destiny, what good and evil we have in us. Only the autumn can show what the spring has sown; only in the evening can we see what the morning began."

Sheer poetry, I thought. Never mind Rachel, I was spell-bound.

Arnold, however, rolled his eyes.

That's another side of Arnold: he resists the highfalutin and won't countenance anything resembling a cliché. Once at the Zürich Institute he pretended to throw up on a visiting lecturer's shoes.

"Give me pap or give me freedom," he said, wiping his mouth. "I can't digest both at once."

"Prof," said Arnold now, "you're clearly from the old school. 'As ye sow, so shall ye reap.' With all due respect, I've been through that mill and it don't cut a lot of ice with me."

I empathized with Arnold. His father had been a preacher, a pillar of the community. In the pulpit he was a beacon of light; at home he was a dark presence, subject to violent moods. When he died he was eulogized and in his parish church the elders put up a plaque to honor his many years of selfless service. As I've said, I tend to take people at face value. Arnold doesn't.

Adam shrugged.

"I am speaking metaphorically, about inner reality, not of what happens in outer life. I am talking about our potential, our inner children, whose limits we at first, naturally, do not know. I am suggesting that only by giving them full rein will we ever know who we are, really. Of course we must also make choices: what to let live and what not to. We are not only individuals; we are also social creatures with responsibilities and commitments. These are the inescapable Janus-faces of life: ourselves and other people. We have only so much energy. What we give to one is not available to the other. We are obliged to choose, and then to accept the consequences."

Sunny stirred and I let her out for her nightly prowl.

"Anyway," grunted Arnold, "personality as the realization of our whole being is an unattainable ideal."

"Ideals are only signposts," put in Norman, "not the goal."

Adam seized on that. "Indeed, Jung said as much."

And from memory he quoted a remark of Jung's that I've used more than once myself:

> The goal is important only as an idea; the essential thing is the *opus* which leads to the goal: *that* is the goal of a lifetime.[12]

I got all excited and whispered to Rachel: "The *opus* is the work we do on ourselves to transmute our leaden personas into golden personalities. That was what the alchemists did, only they projected it all into matter. Jung wrote a lot about the parallels between alchemical operations and individuation—in *Psychology and Alchemy* and *Aion*, not to mention *Mysterium Coniunctionis*. You see, we're all alchemists when we work on ourselves. If I hadn't been so stuck on Kafka I might have done my thesis on it . . ."

Rachel poked me. "Shh, I knew all that."

"But let us not get ahead of ourselves," Adam was saying. "Just as the child must develop in order to be educated, so the personality must begin to sprout before it can be trained. And here, it seems, is where the danger begins."

Out of the corner of my eye I saw J.K. look up. Like most kids her age she tends to be bored by grown-up talk, but intrigued by mystery and danger. She's read everything by Christopher Pike and has dipped into Edgar Allen Poe; she's also written a thriller or two herself.

Adam acknowledged her interest with a nod.

"Young lady, I am referring to the psychologically unpredictable. We don't know how or in what direction the budding personality will develop, and we have learned enough of nature and the world to be somewhat chary of both. Besides, many of us are influenced by the Christian belief that human nature is a blight on the soul, intrinsically evil. Even enlightened psychologists like Freud give us a rather unpleasant picture of the demons that lie slumbering in the depths of the

---

[12] "The Psychology of the Transference," *The Practice of Psychotherapy,* CW 16, par. 400.

human psyche. So it is rather bold to put in a good word for the free and open development of personality."

J.K. went back to her beads.

"Anything might happen," nodded Norman. "Selfishness . . . individualism . . ."

"Indeed," replied Adam, "but individualism is a paper tiger. Individualism is not and never has been a natural development; it is a freakish, impertinent pose that proves its hollowness by crumpling up before the least obstacle. It springs from a belief in the supremacy of individual interests over those of the collective; it means deliberately stressing and giving prominence to some supposed peculiarity rather than to collective considerations and obligations. Let us not confuse that aberrant path with individuality and individuation—the two running mates of personality.

"Individuality refers to the qualities or characteristics that distinguish one person from another. Individuation is self-realization, a process of differentiation and integration, the aim being to become conscious of one's unique psychological reality. Individualism is simply me-first; it leads inexorably to alienation from the collective. The individuating person may of course deviate from collective norms, but all the same retains a healthy respect for them. In Jung's felicitous phrase,

> Individuation does not shut one out from the world, but gathers the world to itself.[13]

"To my mind," added Adam, "the accusation of individualism is a cheap insult when flung at the natural development of personality."

Rachel asked: "What do you think motivates a person to develop personality? I mean instead of settling for persona."

Maybe she was thinking of J.K., who before dinner had confided to us some problems she'd been having around "being herself" and yet being accepted by her friends. I didn't try to reassure our daughter; I was just thrilled she had a conflict.

---

[13] "On the Nature of the Psyche," *The Structure and Dynamics of the Psyche,* CW 8, par. 432.

"Well," said Adam, "it doesn't happen by an act of will, or because somebody says it would be useful or advisable. Nature is not taken in by well-meaning advice. The only thing that moves nature is necessity. Without necessity nothing budges, the human personality least of all. The psyche is tremendously conservative, not to say torpid. The developing personality obeys no caprice, no command, no insight. Only brute necessity will work. Which is to say, we need the motivating force of inner or outer happenings. Anything less would be no better than individualism."

Norman grimaced, perhaps remembering—well, I did—his fateful struggles years ago, which I had been party to.[14]

"You know the expression," said Adam. "Many are called, but few are chosen. I think that's singularly appropriate here, for the development of personality from the germ-state to full consciousness is a curse as well as a gift. That's because its first fruit is the segregation of the individual from the undifferentiated and unconscious herd. This means isolation, and there is no more comforting word for it. Neither family nor society nor position can save one from this fate, nor yet the most successful adaptation to the environment.

"The development of personality, you see, means fidelity to the law of one's own being, and this is a favor that must be paid for dearly. Indeed, the people who talk most loudly about developing their personalities are the very ones who are least mindful of the results, which are such as to frighten away all but the most hardy.

"Personality cannot develop unless the individual chooses his or her own way, consciously and with moral deliberation. And so to the causal motive—necessity—we must therefore add conscious moral decision. If the first is lacking, then the alleged development is merely willful acrobatics; if the second, it will become mechanical and sterile.

"Now, you can make a commitment to go your own way only if you believe that way to be the best. If some other way were held to

---

[14] Norman had come to me for analysis in his late thirties. His situation and what happened to him during our work together is the substance of my *Survival Papers* and *Dear Gladys*.

be better, then you would live and develop that other personality instead of your own. The other ways, of course, are conventionalities of a moral, social, political, philosophical or religious nature, all the well-known isms. The fact that these conventions always flourish in one form or another only proves that the vast majority of mankind do not choose their own way; consequently they develop not themselves but a method and a collective mode of life at the cost of their own wholeness."

"Surely convention is a collective necessity," said Norman.

"Yes," said Adam, "but it is a stopgap and not an ideal, for adherence to it involves renouncing one's wholeness and running away from the consequences of one's own being. The development of personality is a deviation not congenial to the herd, and therefore an unpopular undertaking."

That was a lot to take in, and for some time no one said anything. Finally Arnold spoke.

"Who would willingly set themselves apart?"

Was he being facetious? This man who'd thrown up everything at the peak of a highly paid career? I couldn't tell.

"Only heroes," replied Adam, "those who have historically been looked up to, loved and worshipped, the true sons of God whose names perish not. They are the flower and the fruit, the ever fertile seeds of the tree of humanity. Their greatness lies not in having abjectly submitted to convention, but in their self-deliverance *from* convention. They boldly chose their own way, not in defiance—that would be individualism—but because they were driven to do so by something inside."

More poetry, I loved it.

"The man in the street," said Adam, "has always believed that anyone who would turn aside from the beaten path and strike out on the steep unknown was, if not actually crazy, at least possessed by a demon or a god; the miracle of someone being able to act otherwise than as humanity has always acted could only be explained by the gift of demonic power or divine spirit. That is why, from the beginning, heroes were endowed with god-like attributes."

I remembered some examples. According to Nordic mythology they had snake's eyes, and there was something peculiar about their birth or descent; certain heroes of ancient Greece were snake-souled, others had a personal daemon, were magicians or the elect of God. Only yesterday I had read about the Ojibway folk-hero Nanabozho. Born on an island in Lake Superior, of a spirit from on high and a woman on earth, it is said that his footsteps were so long that he could easily cross the widest river or lake in one stride; he could seize lightning in his bare hands, transform himself into any animal or object of nature, and converse fluently with all living creatures.[15]

"Now we have psychology," said Adam. "On a collective level we still have heroes—athletes, actors, politicians and the like—and some of these we treat like gods. But many among us no longer expect of them anything as elusive and differentiated as personality. Individually, we have raised our sights. Thanks to Jung we now know that personality, in any substantial use of the term, depends upon a harmonious mix of ego, persona and shadow, in helpful alliance with anima or animus, our contrasexual sides, *plus* a working relationship with something greater."

"You mean the Self?" I ventured.

"Yes," said Adam, "the regulating center of the psyche, that unknown force or higher power indistinguishable from what has traditionally been called God, only Jung located it inside. Call it what you want, it monitors our every act and moves us in untold directions. Without the Self we would have to depend on will power. That is not enough to save us from ourselves, nor to make a personality out of a sow's ear; not on your life.

"Remember Chicken Little's dire warning? Oh we had our way with her, and great fun it was, but archetypally speaking she was right. The sky *is* falling, or rather has. Heaven and all we ever projected into it has fallen into the human psyche, with consequences yet to be realized."

Sunny stood and stretched. Adam did the same.

---

[15] See Ella Elizabeth Clark, *Indian Legends of Canada*, p. 5.

"Tomorrow," he said, "granted another day on this earth, I shall pursue with you the enigmatic twists and turns that make psychology what it properly is: a soulful encounter with our parts unknown."

"A mystery?" piped J.-K. "Adventure?"

"You precious child," said Adam, and bid us good-night.

There was a fine sunset, at last. Rachel and I sat on the beach and held hands. The horizon blazed red and blue and yellow, and then slivered into a deep orange band that slowly disappeared.

"I missed you." I said.

My eyes filled. Missed her! My god, I'd been frantic. I'm only half a man without her. From not knowing I had a soul I had come to realize I was lost without one. Not all of this was put on Rachel, but enough.

Rachel sniffed. She's not as sentimental as I am and she's had her fill of projection. Still, she's human.

"How much?" she asked.

"A bushel and a peck."

"And a hug around the neck?"

"If you'll permit."

"Dummy."

Stars came out, the moon, music with strings, the whole shebang. I wrapped us up in a blanket and we played our lovers' harp.

4
Vocation

The next morning dawned bright and clear. Rachel and Adam took off in the canoe. Norman set to work chopping wood and washing the cars. Sunny had chased her quota of squirrels and lay snoozing under a tree. J.K. had found a spade and some plastic sheeting in the shed and was scouting the grounds for a good place to make a pond. Arnold was busy sleeping in.

Alone in the house I immersed myself in Jung's essay on personality. Continuing Adam's line of thought from last night, I read:

> What is it, in the end, that induces a man to go his own way and to rise out of unconscious identity with the mass as out of a swathing mist? Not necessity, for necessity comes to many, and they all take refuge in convention. Not moral decision, for nine times out of ten we decide for convention likewise. What is it, then, that inexorably tips the scales in favour of the *extra-ordinary?*
>
> It is what is commonly called *vocation:* an irrational factor that destines a man to emancipate himself from the herd and from its well-worn paths. True personality is always a vocation and puts its trust in it as in God, despite its being, as the ordinary man would say, only a personal feeling. But vocation acts like a law of God from which there is no escape. The fact that many a man who goes his own way ends in ruin means nothing to one who has a vocation. He *must* obey his own law, as if it were a daemon whispering to him of new and wonderful paths. Anyone with a vocation hears the voice of the inner man: he is *called. . . .*
>
> The original meaning of "to have a vocation" is "to be addressed by a voice." The clearest examples of this are to be found in the avowals of the Old Testament prophets. That it is not just a quaint old-fashioned way of speaking is proved by the confessions of historical personalities such as Goethe and Napoleon . . . who made no secret of their feeling of vocation.[16]

---

[16] *The Development of Personality,* CW 17, pars. 299ff.

When Arnold and I were in Zürich we listened for that voice. Was analytic work truly our vocation? If the voice called, would we hear? What if it didn't? Or, almost worse, what if it did? We were mindful of the way Samuel became one of the elect:

And it came to pass at that time . . . ere the lamp of God went out in the temple of the Lord, where the ark of God was, and Samuel was laid down to sleep;
That the Lord called Samuel: and he answered, Here am I.
And he ran unto Eli, and said, Here am I; for thou calledst me. And he said, I called not; lie down again. And he went and lay down.
And the Lord called yet again, Samuel. And Samuel arose and went to Eli, and said, Here am I; for thou didst call me. And he answered, I called not, my son; lie down again. . . .
And the Lord called Samuel again the third time. And he arose and went to Eli, and said, Here am I; for thou didst call me. And Eli perceived that the Lord had called the child.
Therefore Eli said unto Samuel, Go, lie down: and it shall be, if he call thee, that thou shalt say, Speak, Lord; for thy servant heareth. So Samuel went and lay down in his place.
And the Lord came, and stood, and called as at other times, Samuel, Samuel. Then Samuel answered, Speak; for thy servant heareth.[17]

That's more or less what happened to me. One night, just like Samuel, I distinctly heard my name called, not once but thrice, and then again.

"Speak!" I cried, leaping out of bed, "I do heareth!" and was ripe for holy orders before I heard Arnold snickering in his room.

We had a good old pillow fight then. Kids at heart.

But the laugh was on Arnold. Having already accepted that God— a.k.a. the Self—moves in mysterious ways, it was not a great leap of faith, in fact barely a hippety-hop, to imagine my feckless friend as His unwitting messenger.

Arnold's own call had been more like a shout. After two years at the Institute, he became disenchanted with the curriculum, which he felt was straying from Jung. When they started teaching Winnicott

---

[17] 1 Sam. 3: 2-10, Authorized Version.

and Melanie Klein, Arnold stopped going to lectures. Hans Kohut's self psychology drove him up the wall. With the introduction of psychodrama he became passive-aggressive. When the time came to graduate, he politely accepted his Diploma and then ate it.

Jung goes on:

> Vocation, or the feeling of it, is not, however, the prerogative of great personalities; it is also appropriate to the small ones all the way down to the "midget" personalities, but as the size decreases the voice becomes more and more muffled and unconscious. It is as if the voice of the daemon within were moving further and further off, and spoke more rarely and more indistinctly. The smaller the personality, the dimmer and more unconscious it becomes, until finally it merges indistinguishably with the surrounding society, thus surrendering its own wholeness and dissolving into the wholeness of the group.[18]

Like when you join a political party or get involved in social action. I suppose that wouldn't stop me from thumping the drum or marching in the street if I had a vocation for politics, but I don't do the former because I don't have the latter.

Adam and Rachel came back fresh-faced and radiant. The others were summoned and we had lunch. Rachel whipped up ham omelets and served them with sliced tomatoes in a piquant sesame sauce. J.K., a committed vegetarian, was happy with a plate of cheese-filled perogis and an apple.

"How come you don't eat meat?" asked Arnold, who would sell his soul for a thick juicy steak smothered in onions.

"I don't like the way animals are treated."

"It doesn't change the way they taste," he said.

J.K. knuckled his ear. Or maybe I just thought she should have; when I was her age it was a sign of affectionate exasperation.

"How's the pond coming?" I asked.

"Okay, I guess."

Her brow furrowed.

---

[18] *The Development of Personality,* CW 17, par. 302.

"See, I have this problem. I dug a hole and lined it with plastic. I put rocks and earth in it and filled it with water; then I added duckweed, like the book says. I found some snails and worms; I caught some minnows and crayfish and dumped them in. It looked great! But half an hour later the water was gone."

"Maybe there are holes in the plastic," said Norman. "C'mon, let's see if we can fix it."

Arnold wished them luck and took himself back to bed.

I showed Adam and Rachel what I'd been reading.

" 'The wholeness of the group' . . ." repeated Adam. "Sounds like an oxymoron to me. Perhaps Jung was being ironic. He said himself that the call to become whole is not heard *en masse*. The inner voice is drowned out by convention, and vocation is replaced by collective necessities."

"Doing psychological work with groups was very popular in my time," said Rachel.

"Yes, and it is in the so-called New Age movement," said Adam. "I can understand the value in support groups—people sharing their traumatic experiences. That's abreaction; it's cathartic and it has a place. However, it doesn't go very deep. Apparently there is a widespread desire to change, a genuine search for a transformative experience. There's nothing wrong with that. God knows, if we stay the way we are humanity is doomed. But I'm afraid people tend to mistake temporarily heightened awareness for rebirth. They think they have been forever changed when they are merely inflated with an overdose of previously unconscious material.

"I can tell you, many's the analysand who came to me high as a kite after a weekend workshop and had to be peeled off the wall. Jung acknowledged that one can feel transformed during a group experience, but he cautioned against confusing this with the real thing. The presence of many people together exerts great suggestive force due to the phenomenon of *participation mystique*, unconscious identification, hence the individual in a crowd easily becomes the victim of his or her own suggestibility."

Adam picked up a book. "Here's what Jung wrote":

If any considerable group of persons are united and identified with
one another by a particular frame of mind, the resultant transformation experience bears only a very remote resemblance to the experience of individual transformation. A group experience takes place on
a lower level of consciousness than the experience of an individual.
This is due to the fact that, when many people gather together to
share one common emotion, the total psyche emerging from the
group is below the level of the individual psyche. If it is a very large
group, the collective psyche will be more like the psyche of an animal, which is the reason why the ethical attitude of large organizations is always doubtful. The psychology of a large crowd inevitably
sinks to the level of mob psychology. . . . In the crowd one feels no
responsibility, but also no fear.[19]

"You see," said Adam, "identification with the group is a simple
and easy path to follow, but the group experience goes no deeper
than the level of one's own mind in that state. It may work a change
in you, but the change doesn't last. You have to have continual re-
course to mass intoxication in order to consolidate the experience and
your belief in it.

"Of course positive experiences are also possible. The group can
spur a person to noble deeds or instill a feeling of human solidarity.
That can't be denied. The group can give the individual a degree of
courage, a bearing and a dignity that may easily get lost in isolation.
But in the long run such gifts are unearned. Away from the crowd
and alone, you are a different person and unable to reproduce the
previous state of mind."

"It seems to me," said Rachel, "that those seriously interested in
understanding themselves would have their hands full just dealing
with what happens to them in the course of an ordinary day."

"Alas," sighed Adam, "for many that is too mundane. Group
work and esoteric practices—crystals, vision quests, channeling and
the like—are much more exciting. They tempt with promises none of
us is immune to: deliverance from the woes of this world and escape
from oneself."

---

[19] "Concerning Rebirth," *The Archetypes and the Collective Unconscious,*
CW 9i, par. 225.

Yes, and this had been as true of me as of anyone else. Was I not a lapsed Nirvana seeker? Had I not sought to lose myself in the Oneness of nature in the hills of Zürich? At various times in my life I had sought enlightenment in the study of astrology, graphology, phrenology (bumps on the skull), the Rosicrucians, yoga and existentialism. All interesting enough, but when it came to the crunch they were no help at all.

"Mind you," said Adam, "even under such conditions not a few are called awake by the inner voice. At once they are set apart, feeling themselves confronted with a problem about which the others know nothing. It is not a comfortable situation. In most cases it is impossible to explain what has happened, for understanding is walled off by impenetrable prejudices. 'You are no different from anybody else,' chorus the others, or 'There's no such thing,' and even if they acknowledge the experience it is likely to be branded as morbid or unseemly."

"Or worse," I said, "as purely psychological."

Adam nodded. "That accusation is extremely popular these days. It stems from a curious underestimation of anything psychic, which people apparently regard as personal, arbitrary and therefore futile. And this, paradoxically enough, despite their professed enthusiasm for psychology!"

He banged his fist on the table. Sunny jumped about a foot.

"The unconscious, they say," said Adam, "is, after all, nothing but fantasy. We merely imagine such and such. People think themselves magicians who can conjure the psyche hither and thither and fashion it to suit their moods. They deny what strikes them as inconvenient and sublimate anything nasty; they explain away their phobias and feel in the end that they have arranged everything quite beautifully. Meanwhile they have forgotten the essential point, which is that only the tiniest fraction of the psyche is identical with the conscious mind and its box of magic tricks; much the greater part is sheer unconscious fact, hard as granite, immovable, inaccessible, yet ready at any time to come crashing down upon us at the behest of unseen powers."

I really liked it when Adam got going like that. It was as if Jung himself were in the room; it made the long trip worthwhile.

"But all this is so much abstraction," he continued. "Everyone knows that the intellect, that clever jackanapes, can put it this way or that or any other. It is a very different thing when the psyche, as an objective fact, confronts a man as an inner experience and addresses him in an audible voice: 'This is what will and must be.' Then he feels himself called, just as the group does when there's a war on, or a revolution, or some other madness."

I saw a distinct danger.

"Jung talks about the redeemer personality," I said, "one who hears the call and gets emancipated from the collective. Sure, such persons can be a beacon of hope for others, but aren't they prone to inflation? Isn't that how cults start?"

"Indeed, when the masses feel the tug of psychic forces, they always long for a hero, a slayer of dragons," replied Adam. "The group, because of its unconsciousness, has no freedom of choice, and so psychic activity goes on in it unchecked, like an uncontrolled law of nature. There is thus set going a chain reaction that comes to a stop only in catastrophe. It is not for nothing that our age calls for a redeemer, a potential savior, one who has disidentified from the group psyche—an individual, someone with personality. "

"But what does the individual have to do with the plight of the many?" asked Rachel.

Adam smiled.

"In the first place, he is part of the people as a whole, and is as much at the mercy of the power that moves the whole as anybody else. The only thing that distinguishes him from all the others is his vocation. He has been called by that all-powerful, all-tyrannizing psychic necessity that is his own and his people's affliction. If he hearkens to the voice, he is at once set apart and isolated, as he has resolved to obey the law that commands him from within."

"His own law?" I asked.

"Rather *the* law, the vocation for which he is destined—no more his own than is a load of bricks that might randomly flatten him in the street, but no less either. He is not the master of his own fate. He acquiesces in what the gods have in store or he's done for. If he consciously and intentionally takes on the burden of completeness—heavier than any load of bricks—he avoids all the unhappy consequences of repressed individuation. Which is to say, he won't find it just happening to him against his will.

"Remember Jung's pithy remark?"—and looking at the ceiling Adam quoted one of my all-time favorites:

> Anyone who is destined to descend into a deep pit had better set about it with all the necessary precautions rather than risk falling into the hole backwards.[20]

"He, he," grumbled Rachel. "What about the rest of us?"

For a moment Adam was disconcerted.

"I was speaking generically," he said, "as did Jung."

Rachel flared. Gender language is one of her triggers.

"Generic refers to a class or group with things in common," she said. "Men and women aren't generic."

Adam frowned and looked away. "One could dispute that, though not on biological grounds."

Rachel was half out of her chair.

Adam held his hand up. "Please, I mean no disrespect when I use masculine pronouns to refer to us all—nor, I believe, did Jung. He was a man of his time, as am I. Our collective shadow thrives in linguistic tradition. I do apologize."

Rachel smiled. I returned to my previous point.

"And inflation? Self-styled redeemers?"

Adam pursed his lips.

"Well, I'm afraid inflation is unavoidable, at least at first. Hearing the call is a numinous experience. Such events always have a deep emotional resonance. A hitherto unconscious content has become conscious. What was previously unknown is now known. That automatically results in an enlargement of the personality. Sudden conversions and other far-reaching changes of mind—Paul on the road

---

[20] *Aion,* CW 9ii, par. 125.

to Damascus, my own modest epiphany,[21] to name but two—have their origin in such experiences. Whether for good or ill, however, only time will tell. Consciousness may be temporarily disoriented, and in pathological cases, where the ego is particularly weak, the entire personality may disintegrate."

"Schizophrenia?" asked Rachel.

"Yes, in the extreme. In schizophrenia you have a splitting of the mind, multiple personalities with no central control—a free-for-all among the complexes. Golden apples drop from the same tree, whether they be gathered by a locksmith's apprentice with water on the brain or by a Schopenhauer."

What a bizarre apposition, I thought, as I wrote it down.

"Let me read you some comments by Jung on the subject of inflation," said Adam.

He shuffled through some books and then read:

[Inflation] occurs whenever people are overpowered by knowledge or by some new realization. "Knowledge puffeth up," Paul writes to the Corinthians, for the new knowledge had turned the heads of many, as indeed constantly happens. The inflation has nothing to do with the *kind* of knowledge, but simply and solely with the fact that any new knowledge can so seize hold of a weak head that he no longer sees and hears anything else. He is hypnotized by it, and instantly believes he has solved the riddle of the universe. But that is equivalent to almighty self-conceit. . . . Every step towards greater consciousness is a kind of Promethean guilt: through knowledge, the gods are as it were robbed of their fire, that is, something that was the property of the unconscious powers is torn out of its natural context and subordinated to the whims of the conscious mind. The man who has usurped the new knowledge . . . . has alienated himself from humanity. The pain of this loneliness is the vengeance of the gods, for never again can he return to mankind. He is, as the myth [of Prometheus] says, chained to the lonely cliffs of the Caucasus, forsaken of God and man.[22]

---

[21] See *Chicken Little*, pp. 49ff.
[22] "The Relations Between the Ego and the Unconscious," *Two Essays*, CW 7, par. 243n.

" 'And there an eagle with outstretched wings,' " quoted Arnold, who had just entered the room, " 'did feed upon his immortal liver; as much as was devoured during the day, that much grew again during the night' —that's from Hesiod."

"Thank you," bowed Adam. "Some say Prometheus suffered for 30 years, others 30,000, before being released. Fortunately, few of us have to go through all that. The ancient notion of the liver as the seat of the soul may linger on, but nowadays common sense and the sharp reactions of others to an unwonted lofty attitude, an assumed godlikeness, are usually enough to bring one down to earth."

"There's still the feeling of being set apart, isn't there?" I said.

"Indeed. Anyone who has found his or her individual path is bound to feel estranged from those who haven't. This is simply a particular case of what I have generally observed, that those who have worked on themselves don't care to spend much time with those who haven't."

Rachel squirmed. "That just sounds so elitist."

"Thou sayest," replied Adam. "Nature is aristocratic. In the wild, one animal of value outweighs ten lesser ones. And just so, in daily life, we may prefer to interact with those worth more to us. This may come down to forsaking old friends. Our time on this earth is precious; let us not squander it on those we don't enjoy being with."

Rachel swallowed that, though maybe not whole-hog.

"Listen," said Adam, "to another passage by Jung on inflation":

An inflated consciousness is always egocentric and conscious of nothing but its own existence. It is incapable of learning from the past, incapable of understanding contemporary events, and incapable of drawing right conclusions about the future. It is hypnotized by itself and therefore cannot be argued with. It inevitably dooms itself to calamities that must strike it dead. Paradoxically enough, inflation is a regression of consciousness into unconsciousness. This always happens when consciousness takes too many unconscious contents upon itself and loses the faculty of discrimination, the *sine qua non* of all consciousness.[23]

---

[23] *Psychology and Alchemy,* CW 12, par. 563.

"Inflation," summarized Adam, "is a phenomenon that involves an extension of the personality beyond individual limits. This regularly happens in analysis, as ego-awareness lights up the dark, but it is common in everyday life as well.

"One instance is the humorless way in which people identify themselves with their business or title. The office I hold may certainly be my special activity, but it is also a collective factor that exists primarily and historically on account of the cooperation of many others; thus its dignity rests solely on collective approval. When I identify with my office or title, I am inclined to behave as if I myself were the whole complex of social factors of which that office consists—as though I were not only the bearer of the office, but also and at the same time had the personal approval of society. This is an extraordinary extension of myself; I have usurped qualities that do not belong to me but come from outside. *L'état c'est moi* is the motto for such people."

I was digesting all that when Arnold spoke.

"Prof, on the level now, do you think there's anything at all to be said for being unconscious?"

Adam's eyes sparkled. Thinking of the Niederdorf? I was.

"As a matter of fact," he said, "becoming too conscious can take much of the fun out of life. In the formative years—until the late thirties, say—unconsciousness is not necessarily unhealthy; it permits a variety of experiences that later will be the *prima materia,* the grist, for analysis . . . And even when older, it is often necessary to regress, to become unconscious, in order to find out who you are. Act first and work on it later! I have often said as much to those fearful of life. But of course that's only in the short run. In the long run, as Jung said so succinctly":

> The reason why consciousness exists, and why there is an urge to widen and deepen it, is very simple: without consciousness things go less well.[24]

---

[24] "Analytical Psychology and *Weltanschauung,*" *The Structure and Dynamics of the Psyche,* CW 8, par. 695.

"I can speak to that," said Norman quietly.

He had crept in unnoticed.

"Twenty-five years ago," said Norman, "I was a hippy. I took a train across the country to San Francisco where I partied for a month. Fineglow was the name I gave my home-grown grass. I smoked it all the way, stoned the whole time. And everyone I met was too. Then I sat in a window seat near the corner of Haight and Ashbury and blew my mind on Janis Joplin and Joe Cocker and Bob Dylan. I ate magic mushrooms with artists and felt like a king. I went into the Oregon hills and shot a deer. I mingled with beautiful people and felt great just being alive. Time was electric."

"So?" said Rachel.

"So it sapped my energy," replied Norman. "I became indolent and oblivious to reality. There was nothing I couldn't do, but I didn't *need* to do anything. I floated from place to place, moment to moment. Anything was possible, anything acceptable. Whatever was happenin', man, was okay—I went with the flow. I felt like a god and I behaved like one. That's my experience of inflation. There's no substance to a life like that. It's all air!"

"You're pretty worked up about it," observed Rachel.

"I was a puer," said Norman simply. "I felt creative, but I didn't create. I felt beautiful, but I did ugly things. I felt invulnerable, but I hurt a lot."

He glanced my way. Yes, I remembered his guilt and his tearful lament, that he paid a high price for a meager return: "I disappointed those who depended on me, people I loved." At the same time, what he learned about himself was pure gold. Could he have had one without the other? Was his crisis a result of being unconscious? Or did the Self engineer a crisis so that he'd grow up?

"Puer psychology," mused Rachel. "Give me a minute."

She left the room. We cooled our heels with small talk about the weather, up-coming elections, the stock market and so on, none of which any of us had much knowledge about.

Rachel returned with a book. "Here's how a novelist describes her experience of puers":

Fay knew about men who wouldn't grow up, and she wished she could tell Lizzie [her daughter], warn her. But she knew Lizzie wouldn't listen any more than she had listened.

A man like this is so wildly attractive, so maddeningly alive, that he is absolutely irresistible. In the Tarot deck, he is the Fool . . . .

In the picture on the card, the Fool, like a hobo, carries a sack tied to a stick. They leave you, these men, but they never said they were staying, never said they were committed, or purposeful—or responsible, even. All they want is to have a good time. And what's wrong with that? Nothing, except you begin to wonder how interested *you* are in having a good time. . . .

The joy of being with these men is the giddy return, through them, to a child's world, where there are no clocks and no claims on your time, no clothes to be kept clean, and no consequences to be considered. Days and nights are filled with the silliness, the spontaneity, the conspiratorial privacy, and all the breathless secret pleasures of life in a tree house. . . .

They don't always come home, and they won't even apologize for it. They won't help around the house because they like it all messed up. They won't work very hard because they don't want to get trapped by success. And they won't work at the relationship because it's not supposed to be work, it's supposed to be fun. If you don't want to play with them, they don't mind. But that isn't going to stop them from playing.

Somehow, they make you feel very old, these men. They turn you into their mother.[25]

"Uh-huh," nodded Norman. "That's about how my wife Nancy put it at the time. Maybe I should have thanked her."

"Anyone hungry?" asked Adam.

After tea and tarts, Norman and J.K. went back to the pond. Rachel got out her sketchbook. I conferred with Arnold and then addressed our host.

"Adam," I said, "would you mind saying more about the idea of collective redemption via a hero or savior?"

"Not at all," he said. "With the conscious decision to put one's own way above all other possible ways, one has already fulfilled the

---

[25] Marsha Norman, *The Fortune Teller,* pp. 116-117.

greater part of one's vocation as a redeemer. With other ways invalidated and one's personal truth exalted above convention, there is a clean sweep, as it were, of all those things that not only failed to prevent the great danger, but actually accelerated it."

"What great danger?" I queried.

"I was thinking," said Adam, "of the collapse of the persona—breakdown, the disruption of life as it has been known. Conventions in themselves are soulless mechanisms that can never understand more than the mere routine of life. For those who are called to something more, that is not enough."

Arnold asked: "Doesn't the creative life always stand outside convention?"

"There you have it," nodded Adam. "That is why, when the mere routine of life predominates in the form of convention and tradition—doing the right thing, putting your best foot forward and so on—there is bound to be a destructive outbreak of creative energy."

"Creative energy . . . destructive?" said Rachel, looking up.

"Destruction is the dark side of any energy that is repressed," said Adam. "We are all potentially creative, and I don't mean artistic. But come to that, what is art? The American painter Robert Henri objected to the nineteenth-century definition of art as a thing beautifully done. Let us dispense with the adverb, he suggested; things are not done beautifully, their beauty is simply an integral part of their having been done. In that sense, anyone who makes or does something is an artist. And why not? Art is not a monopoly of those with a particular talent, nor is it necessarily an external thing; it is a natural outcome of a state of being."

Adam paced.

"We all have God-given gifts—our innate potential. Those who are not involved in exploring their own possibilities, their individual talents, will take their frustration out on others or on themselves, and often on both. Relationships suffer, health deteriorates. Heart and liver ailments, skin problems, kidney disease, cancer, depression and conflict, these are all concomitants of undeveloped potential. I don't say that the latter causes the former, or vice versa—I am no doctor and the body has its own laws, after all—but they have been observed to go together. Here's what Jung says":

> This outbreak [of creative energy] is a catastrophe only when it is a mass phenomenon, but never in the individual who consciously submits to these higher powers and serves them with all his strength. The mechanism of convention keeps people unconscious, for in that state they can follow their accustomed tracks like blind brutes, without the need for conscious decision. . . . Then, just as with animals, panic is liable to break out among human beings kept unconscious by routine, and with equally predictable results.[26]

Another rant, I noted gleefully.

"Personality, however," said Adam, "does not allow itself to be seized by the panic that smites those who are just waking to consciousness, for it has put all its terrors behind it. Those who have achieved personality are able to cope with the changing times, and have unknowingly and involuntarily become leaders."

Arnold, no more comfortable with leading than being led, shook his head. He'd returned from Zürich a hero—well, to some eyes, including mine—but he'd laughed off the mantle of guru and done his own thing. Soon, in spite of himself, he had followers. Some were imitators, but never mind, Arnold wasn't happy with either.

"I am not keen on being a model for others," he said.

Adam laughed.

"My dear sir, that is not your choice. Simply and naturally, by virtue of the work on yourself, you are a magnet for those whose souls long for life. Granted, this is not your problem, but you do have to own up to the person you've become. Who you are, whether you will or no, has an inductive effect on others. To my mind this is all to the good, for if enough individuals become more conscious, why then the collective will too and life on this earth will go on.

"Let me suggest to you a guiding principle: Be the man through whom you wish to influence others. Mere talk is hollow. There is no trick, however artful, by which this simple truth can be evaded in the

---

[26] "The Development of Personality," *The Development of Personality,* CW 17, par. 305

long run. The fact of being convinced, and not the things we are convinced of, that is what has always, and at all times, worked."

Arnold flinched, and I must say that I too heard these words with something of a shock.

I remembered at university having to write an essay on the ethical consequences of aberrant—defined as unconventional—thought and/ or behavior. Plato? Socrates? I don't remember the context. I do recall the instruction to grapple with the question, "What if everyone thought or acted as you do?"—and my feeling at the time: little me among so many, what's to worry?

That was almost forty years ago. Now, in the psychological terms presented by Adam, I could not deny a collective responsibility for what I did and thought. I won't say it hadn't occurred to me before, but then it isn't the kind of thing likely to haunt introverted sensation types anyway.

"All human beings are much alike," Adam was saying, "otherwise we could not succumb to the same delusions. The psychic substratum upon which individual consciousness is based—I mean the collective unconscious, the objective psyche—is universally the same, otherwise people could never reach a common understanding. In this sense, personality and its peculiar psychic make-up are not something absolutely unique. The uniqueness holds only for the *individual* nature of the personality, assuming it is discovered."

"And that's not the prerogative of genius," observed Rachel.

"Dear lady, you are quite right. One may be a genius without being a personality, or the other way around. In fact, in my experience the latter is more the rule: few personalities are intellectual giants. Since every individual has an inborn law of life to answer to, it is theoretically possible for anyone to follow this law and so become a personality, that is, to achieve wholeness.

"Mental prowess is but a minor component of personality, nor is it a significant factor in individuation. Indeed, in fairy tales, where so many psychic patterns are illustrated, the one who finds the treasure —the key, the gold, the princess—is as often as not a Dummling, an innocent fool."

I glanced at Arnold. His eyes were closed.

"The primary question in speaking of personality, as of individuation," said Adam, "is always, 'Are you living your own way?' Of course a degree of consciousness is necessary in order to know the answer, and that, essentially, is the treasure the Dummling seeks."

I leafed back a few pages.

"Adam, you said earlier that those who lack a persona—'innocents abroad,' your words—are a sorry lot. How does that square with Dummling-ness?"

Adam smoothed his pate.

"Well, on the surface, not easily."

And he fell silent, just like when we were in the canoe.

I looked around. Rachel was still there, thank goodness. So was Sunny, eyes closed, nose resting on my foot. I didn't panic but I did cross my fingers.

"My feeling," said Adam at last, "is that the Dummling in fairy tales represents an aspect of the individual psyche that has not been coerced by collective pressures. We all had it at first, and still do, though buried under the accretions of daily life—a virgin innocence unhobbled by hard knocks: fresh, spontaneous and not yet fixed in rigid patterns. That openness to the unknown, naiveté if you like, is what is constellated in the struggle to discover our own individual truth. Only the one who can consciously assent to the power of this inner voice becomes a personality.

"The great and liberating thing about any genuine personality is that you voluntarily sacrifice yourself to the call, and consciously translate into individual reality what would only lead to ruin if it were lived unconsciously by the group."

That was deep. I was mulling it over when Norman burst in.

"Come quick!"

We rushed out the door, Sunny and Arnold too. We tailed Norman and came upon J.K. looking pleased as punch. She had planted a flag beside her pond.

"Voila! *Moi* did it!"

It looked like a professional job. The border was trimmed with rocks and bark and it was teaming with life. A green blanket of duck-weed covered the surface. Frogs sunned themselves on twigs. The flag was a white rag with big black letters:

AGAINST
ANIMAL TESTING

Adam surveyed the scene. He bent down and stirred the murky water, then licked his finger.

"Good soup!" he exclaimed. "I would give it A-plus. Tell that to your teachers."

J.K. glowed.

Arnold and Norman clapped and I gave her a special hug. Sunny barked. Rachel beamed as if it were all her doing; they're that close.

Back in the A-frame, Adam resumed his narrative as he scrubbed vegetables for the evening meal.

"Life only exists in the form of living units, that is, individuals; the law of life always tends toward a life individually lived. So although the objective psyche can only be conceived as a universal and uniform datum, which means we all share the same primary, psychic condition, it must nevertheless individuate if it is to become actualized, for there is no other way in which it could express itself except through the individual human being.

"The only exception to this is when the objective psyche seizes hold of a group, in which case it must, of its own nature, precipitate a catastrophe, because in that context it can only operate unconsciously and is not assimilated by individual consciousness or assigned its place among the existing conditions of life."

Rachel scoured the fridge and found the makings of a salad. Arnold was picking burrs off Sunny. Norman and J.K. debated the relative merits of zoom lenses and fixed-focus telephotos. I set the table and listened.

"This thing we call personality is a great and mysterious problem," said Adam. "Everything that can be said about it is curiously unsatisfactory and inadequate, and there is always a danger of the discussion losing itself in pomposity and empty chatter. The very idea of personality, in common usage, is so vague and ill-defined that one hardly ever finds two people who understand the word in the same sense."

Rachel nodded as she filled Adam's foot-high pepper grinder. I opened a bottle of plonk rusting in the cupboard.

"Jung puts forward a more definite, and to my mind more satisfactory, concept of personality," continued Adam, "but I don't imagine he has uttered the last word. He himself cautioned his readers that everything he said on the subject was only a tentative attempt to approach the problem; he didn't claim to have solved it."

"My reading of Jung's essay on personality," I said, "is that it is an apt description of the problems faced by anyone who dares to deviate from the collective way. All the usual explanations fall short, just as they do with the creative artist."

"My feelings to a tee," said Rachel.

"Of course Jungian psychology has never claimed to explain the artist," observed Adam, "only to interpret the product, which, if it is good enough, evokes a timeless—let us say archetypal—meaning that resonates in the viewer, albeit in individual ways."

"*À table,*" he called, and we all sat down.

Adam served a thick concoction of mixed vegetables and chick peas. Rachel passed around her salad and a ribboned basket of warm garlic bread. I poured the wine.

"Miss Jessy Kate," said Adam, "as the youngest at the table, would you like to say grace?"

J.K. looked at him like he was from another planet.

"Grace who?"

"You precious child, it is a long-standing custom to thank our Maker and bless the food we eat before partaking."

J.K. shrugged. "Oh, that."

She's Jewish, not Orthodox but all the same proud of it. A blessing before a meal was not new to her, only she called it *hamotzi.*

J.K. bowed her head. The rest of us followed suit, except for Sunny, who'd already wolfed down her prescribed portion of Pro

Plan Light ("for overweight, less active, older dogs") and was out in the night scavenging for something more substantial.

"Dear God and Goddess," said J.K., ". . . bless this food and me and my best friend Lalu and everybody else too . . . and please save animals from being cooped up and tortured to make cosmetics and toothpaste and other things."

She paused.

"And help my Dad to stop smoking."

"Amen," said Adam. "Dig in."

5

The Child

"You precious child."

Adam's words echoed in my mind all night. I tossed and turned and dreamed I was flying. Straight up, straight down. Then soaring over roofs and tree-tops, joyfully airborne until I crash-landed in a thicket. I awoke with a start and for a long time lay staring into the night. About 4 a.m. I sidled out of bed and tiptoed downstairs.

I sat at the living room table overlooking the lake. The moon was out, the water calm. Sunny moved out of the shadows and sniffed me. I rubbed her head and gave her a cookie. She slunk back to her favorite spot under the stairs. There was a chill in the air, so I put a log on the dying embers and fanned them into flame.

"You precious child."

There are many ways to hear those words. I could have taken them objectively—Jessy *was* precious to me—but I have learned that whenever I become obsessed with a particular image, more than likely it has something to do with myself.

Further, since it was the second time Adam had addressed J.K. in that way, I took it as a living example of the so-called doubling motif, which Marie-Louise von Franz, interpreting its occurrence in dreams and fairy tales, sees as a content of the unconscious on the brink of becoming conscious. In the unconscious there is no conflict between opposites because everything is one, but at the threshold of consciousness the opposites fall apart.[27] In plainer words, the doubling motif presages a new insight.

What was up? I thought. What was I about to realize?

I always get excited when something new is in the works—that's Arnold's influence, I never used to—but before exploring the signifi-

---

[27] See *On Divination and Synchronicity: The Psychology of Meaningful Chance,* pp. 105-108.

cance of the child subjectively, in terms of my own psychology, I thought I'd like to review what Jung had to say about actual children. I switched on the table lamp and dug out his essay called "Child Development and Education." I came upon this:

> During the first years of life there is hardly any consciousness, though the existence of psychic processes manifests itself at a very early stage. These processes, however, are not grouped round an organized ego; they have no centre and therefore no continuity, lacking which a conscious personality is impossible. Consequently the child has in our sense no memory, despite the plasticity and susceptibility of its psychic organ. Only when the child begins to say "I" is there any perceptible continuity of consciousness. But in between there are frequent periods of unconsciousness. One can actually see the conscious mind coming into existence through the gradual unification of fragments.[28]

J.K., home birth and all, was a holy terror when she was three going on four. Rachel and I agonized over what we'd done wrong. "Parents for the most part are incompetent"—that's what Adam said the other day; it galled at the time, but in all conscience I couldn't exempt myself. Anyway, when J.K. was five her moods leveled out. By the age of six she was almost human, and in the last few years her fragments seemed to be coming together. I read on:

> This process continues throughout life, but from puberty onwards it becomes slower, and fewer and fewer fragments of the unconscious are added to consciousness. . . . In this way the conscious rises out of the unconscious like an island newly risen from the sea. We reinforce this process in children by education and culture. School is in fact a means of strengthening in a purposeful way the integration of consciousness.[29]

Yes, I nodded, and was struck by another thought: could J.K.'s interest in ponds be symbolic of a Self-driven urge to consciously contain a portion of the sea, the vast unconscious? Fanciful, perhaps, but consistent with a developing ego.

---

[28] *The Development of Personality,* CW 17, par. 103.
[29] Ibid.

Jung continues:

> Just as the child in embryo is practically nothing but a part of the mother's body, and wholly dependent on her, so in early infancy the psyche is to a large extent part of the maternal psyche, and will soon become part of the paternal psyche as well. The prime psychological condition is one of fusion with the psychology of the parents, an individual psychological being only potentially present. Hence it is that the nervous and psychic disorders of children right up to school age depend very largely on disturbances in the psychic world of the parents. All parental difficulties reflect themselves without fail in the psyche of the child, sometimes with pathological results. [Thus] the dreams of small children often refer more to the parents than to the child itself.[30]

So maybe J.K.'s early behavior patterns reflected my inner turmoil at the time; I remembered a number of dreams of hers that I'd been obliged to interpret as my own. And it did seem that she had settled down since my relationship with Rachel had become more grounded.

Dear Rachel, anima or flesh-and-blood lover? After all our time together, I still can't easily tell them apart. It's especially confusing when they have the same name.

I sighed. How difficult it is, I thought, to differentiate between who's who once you're aware of an inner life. It's possible, and certainly necessary; it's just not easy.

A hand fell on my shoulder. I gave a start and looked up to see reflected in the window a ghostlike figure hovering behind me. It was Adam in his Ebenezer Scrooge night-shirt and a tasseled bonnet that hung to his waist.

"I couldn't sleep," he said.

I greeted Adam's sudden appearance with ambivalence. I knew his help could be invaluable, but I'd just as soon struggle along on my own until I got the message. However, I couldn't very well dismiss him. It was his own living room, after all. I was more the interloper than he.

---

[30] Ibid., par. 106.

So with some reluctance, speaking quietly so as not to wake the house, I told him what was afoot.

Adam heard me out and then took off on his own hobby-horse. He pointed out that the experience of school is the first impact of the greater world on the child, and said its primary purpose should be to free the child from the parental environment.

"Don't imagine," he said, "that the methodical teaching of a curriculum is paramount. The most important thing is the personality of the teacher. The child, boy or girl, projects onto the teacher, male or female, the father-image, because the father, archetypally, represents the world at large."

"What about working mothers?" I asked.

"Naturally," said Adam, "they have a father-type influence, but don't forget the essentially conservative nature of the psyche. Whatever the individual circumstances, the mother's archetypal role is to care for and nourish. In school, away from hearth and home, the child is at the mercy of the father world. Moreover, if the personal relationship of child to teacher is a good one, it matters very little whether the method of teaching is the most up to date. Success doesn't depend on the method, any more than it does on stuffing children's heads with knowledge."

"But aren't they in school to learn?"

I'm a child of the forties. In those days, if you hadn't learned what had been taught you failed a grade and bad on you.

Adam knit his brow. "Yes, but to learn what?"

I fumbled. "History? Geography? The three R's?"

"Those things may be taught," said Adam, "and they can be echoed back by rote. But learning them is out of our hands. In any case, we need not be overly concerned with the amount of specific information a child learns, or not, at school. The inquiring mind, like water, finds its own level. Reading, writing and arithmetic are important skills, without which one will certainly have a difficult time in the world, but the thing of most vital importance is that school should succeed in freeing the young person from unconscious identity with the family, and thereby contribute toward the growth of in-

dividual consciousness. Without such consciousness, one is doomed
to remain dependent and imitative, feeling misunderstood and suppressed, unwittingly victimized by a collectively acceptable persona."
Thud.

Adam seemed so sure of himself, and I was inclined to agree. But
I had to wonder, and not for the first time, if he had simply hooked
my father complex.

I've always been drawn to those who speak with authority. As a
young man I used to fantasize the existence of a Great Book contain-
ing the answers to all of life's questions, A to Z. Whenever you had
a problem you could just look it up—well, given a decent index—
and find the solution. I subsequently projected such wisdom onto a
number of wizards of Oz, and now I'm wary. Hence, among other
things, my ambivalent attitude toward Adam: I respect his views but
at the same time I'm skeptical.

I faced him squarely.

"You speak with conviction, but how do I know it's the truth?"

Adam tossed his tassels.

"Dear boy, I speak only of what I believe to be true, gleaned from
the work on myself and what I've read in an attempt to make sense
of my experience. As far as I know, nothing is absolute. You must
find your own truth."

I expected no more, but still I felt disappointed. Like most people,
I suppose, I live by a few working truths; hard won, to be sure, but
not much help when I come up against something completely new. I
still long for the big A. Given one objective, unvarying truth, a North
Star of the soul, so to speak, I reckon I could die happy.

The clock struck seven as J.K. came down the stairs, rubbing her
eyes. Like Dante's Beatrice, I thought, but in reverse.

"Hi Dad, I heard voices. What are you doing?"

She sat on my knee and I hugged her.

"A good question," I said.

By the time we finished breakfast it had begun to spit rain. J.K.
donned a slicker and rubber boots and set off with a net and a pail.

"A-hunting I do go," she sang, "for minnows, frogs and snails. I will not rest till I succeed, through rain or hail or gales."

"Write if you get work," I said, "and take Sunny."

We grown-ups sat around the table drinking decaf and discussing the vagaries of education.

"It is pointless," said Adam, "to speak of educating the young without a substantial focus on the education of those who teach. Unfortunately, the psychological state of educators is not a professional issue. Consequently the young are forever at the mercy of the unresolved complexes of those in charge."

Rachel mused: "What about personal analysis as a requirement for a teaching diploma?"

"My dear," smiled Adam, "if it were in my power I would certainly make it mandatory."

This possibility seemed so utterly unlikely that no one spoke, not even Arnold.

Adam helped himself to another cuppa. Two scoops of sugar and double cream, damn the cholesterol.

"Educating teachers is only a specific case of the general problem of educating anybody," he said. "We harbor the quaint notion that a person's education is finished when leaving school, even at the university level. We educate people up to the point where they can earn a living and marry; then formal education ceases, as though a complete mental outfit had been acquired. The solution to all the complicated problems of life is left to the discretion, and alas the ignorance, of the individual.

"Many ill-advised and unhappy marriages, and innumerable professional disappointments, are due solely to the lack of adult education. There should be not only continuation courses for young people, but continuation schools for adults in their prime."

"They do exist," I said, thinking of night school and the like.

Adam waved his hand.

"I am not referring to the acquisition of mental or manual skills, but to the understanding of oneself. Vast numbers of men and women spend their lives in complete ignorance of their own psychology.

To mitigate this, a knowledge of typology, at the very least, would be absolutely essential. The fact that most people don't know who they are or what they're suited for is a travesty with far-reaching practical consequences."

"I took a type test once," said Norman. "It suggested I would do well as a stockbroker."

Adam smiled.

"Dear boy, perhaps that was one of your possible paths. But I suspect it was an aptitude test you took, or perhaps an interest inventory. Aptitude is a measure of what you're good at; typology gives you a handle on the way you function no matter what you do. Using Jung's model, which as you know describes the characteristic parameters of the thinking, sensation, feeling and intuitive functions, any of which may manifest through an introverted or extraverted attitude, we can orient ourselves psychologically as completely as when we locate a place geographically by latitude and longitude. On any journey we need a compass, no less on one of self-discovery.

"I think aptitude can be measured fairly accurately, and at an early age too, but to my mind typology is not something that can be tested with any accuracy. Tests don't show the extent to which one's type may have been falsified by familial and other environmental factors. They say nothing about how the way one functions may be distorted by complexes, and they don't reflect the ever-present compensating attitude of the unconscious. On top of all that, they don't take into account the dynamic nature of the psyche and therefore the possibility of change."

I was glad to hear this, for I knew my own typology had varied over time.[31] For one thing, in university and at P & G I was the life of the party. Just look at me now.

---

[31] Hence in my book on the subject I gave short shrift to tests as a tool for self-knowledge: "The bottom line is that an externally evaluated test, even though self-administered, is not a reliable guide to what is going on inside. In the area of typology, as with any attempt to understand oneself, there is no substitute for prolonged reflection." *(Personality Types: Jung's Model of Typology,* p. 94)

Rachel said, "There are those who believe it isn't possible to educate the adult mind."

"So I've heard," replied Adam. "I see it rather as a slate begging to be written on, throughout life."

"That sounds a lot like Jung," smiled Norman.

"I'm not surprised," said Adam. "I dare say I haven't had an original thought since I was a toddler."

Rachel stifled a laugh.

"Pardon me," she said, "I had a sudden image of the eminent Professor Brillig in diapers. Sorry."

Adam shrugged. "On the other hand, I have carefully screened my psychological mentors, and Jung, to me, makes the most sense."

I was half inclined to let matters rest there. It had stopped raining and the sun was out. I could leave them all and go for a swim. Maybe I'd invite Rachel to join me, just for the fun of it. It wasn't so easy to find time alone in this crowd, and we'd been apart for quite awhile. I felt the stirring of Dionysus.

But my blessèd Apollonian mind would not give way. I pressed Adam and he picked up an earlier thread.

"In educating children," he said, "as already discussed, we must realize that for the most part they are the psychic product of their parents. The child who enters school at five or six is endowed with the nucleus of ego-consciousness, but is incapable of asserting his or her unconscious individuality. One is often tempted to interpret children who are disobedient or difficult to handle as willful or deliberately obstinate. This is a mistake. In such cases we should first examine the parental milieu and family history. Invariably we will discover in the parents valid reasons for the child's peculiarities, which turn out to be far less the expression of an individual disposition than a reflection of disturbing influences in the home.

"Thus, inevitably, the focus falls on the family atmosphere and the psychic state of the parents: their problems, the way they live, the aspirations they have fulfilled or neglected, and so on. All these things profoundly influence the child, who in the early years lives in a state of *participation mystique* with the parents. You can see the infectious nature of the parents' complexes from the effect their mannerisms have on their children. Even when the parents make a mighty effort to control themselves, the children get wind of what's going on. This happens via the unconscious, a consequence of the archaic identity between parent and child."

Arnold hunched forward.

"I once worked with a middle-aged woman who had had a devoted mother," he said. "They were very close, but since puberty this woman had suffered horrible recurring dreams of her mother as a witch or a dangerous animal. She couldn't understand them at all. The daughter came to me when the mother, then in her seventies, began crawling around on all fours, howling like a wolf. She was pronounced insane; lycanthropy, I believe it's called. My analysand wondered about the effect on herself of her mother's latent psychosis, and why she hadn't been aware of it."

Adam nodded.

"Individual consciousness frees itself only gradually from the state of identity with the parents. Often it never happens, or only after the parents are long gone. In the case you mention, one must applaud the daughter for realizing that her mother's underlying problems might have had unrealized consequences for herself."

"As they did, and all bad," frowned Arnold.

"Indeed," said Adam. "Though it is a grave misfortune for a child to have no parents, it is equally dangerous to be too closely bound to them. An excessive attachment to the family is a severe handicap in later adaptation to the world, for a growing human being cannot forever remain a child. That may seem self-evident, but unfortunately many parents keep their children infantile because they themselves don't wish to grow old or give up their parental authority and power. The result is dependent personalities, or independence achieved only precipitately or by furtive means."

"Street kids," observed Norman.

"And street adults," said Arnold.

"For instance," agreed Adam.

I was enjoying this and could see it might go on for hours. But now I was anxious to learn more about the symbolic significance of the child. I therefore excused myself and in privacy—under the eaves, actually, where bat droppings mingled with pink insulating fiber—I browsed through Jung's essay, "The Psychology of the Child Archetype."

Jung begins with an exposition on the general nature of the archetypes—"myth-forming structural elements" in the psyche, he calls them—with a bow to the pioneering work of Carus and Eduard von Hartmann in discovering the existence of the unconscious. He goes on to describe some primordial images or motifs, arising from the presence of archetypes, found in all cultures everywhere, as well as in dreams and fantasies.

Among such motifs is that of the child, representing an instinctive link with our naive past. According to Jung, when we lose touch with our roots, we run the risk of becoming neurotic. He writes:

> We can never legitimately cut loose from our archetypal foundations unless we are prepared to pay the price of a neurosis, any more than we can rid ourselves of our body and its organs without committing suicide. If we cannot deny the archetypes or otherwise neutralize them, we are confronted, at every new stage in the differentiation of consciousness to which civilization attains, with the task of finding a new *interpretation* appropriate to this stage, in order to connect the life of the past that still exists in us with the life of the present, which threatens to slip away from it.[32]

If this link-up doesn't take place, says Jung, a kind of rootless consciousness comes into being no longer oriented to the past, a consciousness that succumbs helplessly to all manner of suggestions and, in practice, is susceptible to psychic epidemics.

> With the loss of the past, now become "insignificant," devalued, and incapable of revaluation, the saviour is lost too . . . . Over and over again in the "metamorphosis of the gods" he [the savior, the way out] rises up as the prophet or first-born of a new generation and

---

[32] *The Archetypes and the Collective Unconscious,* CW 9i, par. 267.

appears unexpectedly in the unlikeliest places (sprung from a stone, tree, furrow, water, etc.) and in ambiguous form.[33]

Hence the multitudinous images of the child that manifest in the therapy of neurosis—Tom Thumbs, dwarfs, elves and such.

Often the child is formed after the Christian model; more often, though, it develops from earlier, altogether non-Christian levels— that is to say, out of chthonic animals such as crocodiles, dragons, serpents, or monkeys. Sometimes the child appears in the cup of a flower, or out of a golden egg, or as the centre of a mandala. In dreams it often appears as the dreamer's son or daughter or as a boy, youth, or young girl. . . . As a special instance of "the treasure hard to attain" motif, the child motif is extremely variable and assumes all manner of shapes, such as the jewel, the pearl, the flower, the chalice, the golden egg, the quaternity, the golden ball, and so on.[34]

Ha! I was on track. My precious child had many parallels.

Statements like "The child motif is a vestigial memory of one's own childhood" and similar explanations merely beg the question. But if, giving this proposition a slight twist, we were to say, "The child motif is a picture of certain *forgotten* things in our childhood," we are getting closer to the truth.[35]

Well . . . I wasn't. My years of analysis had dredged up a lot that I'd forgotten. It was helpful at the time, but I wasn't about to do it again. Jung goes on:

Since, however, the archetype is always an image belonging to the whole human race and not merely to the individual, we might better put it this way: "The child motif represents the pre-conscious, childhood aspect of the collective psyche."[36]

No closer, I'm afraid. But wait, here's something:

Certain phases in an individual's life can . . . personify themselves to the extent that they result in a *vision of oneself*—for instance, one sees oneself as a child. Visionary experiences of this kind,

---

[33] Ibid.
[34] Ibid., par. 270.
[35] Ibid., par. 273.
[36] Ibid.

whether they occur in dreams or in the waking state, are, as we know, conditional on a dissociation having previously taken place between past and present. Such dissociations come about because of various incompatibilities; for instance, a man's present state may have come into conflict with his childhood state, or he may have violently sundered himself from his original character in the interests of some arbitrary persona more in keeping with his ambitions. He has thus become unchildlike and artificial, and has lost his roots. All this presents a favourable opportunity for an equally vehement confrontation with the primary truth.[37]

Had I gone off the rails in favor of an ambitious persona? Had I become artificial? Maybe the "primary truth" was just what I'd been looking for—the big A! I have never liked vehement confrontations, but I suppose I could weather another.

Jung goes on to describe the function of the child archetype:

The child motif represents not only something that existed in the distant past but also something that exists *now* . . . . [Its] purpose is to compensate or correct, in a meaningful manner, the inevitable one-sidednesses and extravagances of the conscious mind. It is in the nature of the conscious mind to concentrate on relatively few contents and to raise them to the highest pitch of clarity. A necessary result and precondition is the exclusion of other potential contents of consciousness. . . . [which] is bound to bring about a certain one-sidedness. . . . [This] is a source of endless transgressions against one's instincts. . . . Our progressiveness, though it may result in a great many delightful wish-fulfilments, piles up an equally gigantic Promethean debt which has to be paid off from time to time in the form of hideous catastrophes. For ages man has dreamed of flying, and all we have got for it is saturation bombing! . . . Our differentiated consciousness is in continual danger of being uprooted; hence it needs compensation through the still existing state of childhood.[38]

So, over and above my natural feeling for J.K., was my interest in her preciousness a self-regulatory attempt by the psyche to compensate for my loss of roots? What was I projecting onto her?

These were certainly big Q's.

---

37 Ibid., par. 274.
38 Ibid., par. 276.

Mind buzzing, I returned to the living room. Arnold was snoring on the couch. Norman and Rachel were discussing the making of bread and how best to can plums.

"Where's Adam?" I asked.

"He took the canoe out," said Rachel.

I fretted.

Twenty minutes later Adam came in, soaking wet.

"Damn piece of plastic!" he said, shrugging out of his life-jacket. "It threw me over."

After he had changed I invited him onto the deck. Ensconced in lawn chairs, high noon approaching, I put it to him.

"Look, I think I'm on to something here, but I'd like your help."

I outlined my thoughts.

Adam toweled his wisps and reflected.

"The child is potential future," he said. "Hence the occurrence of the child motif in the psychology of an individual usually signifies an anticipation of future events. Life is a flux, a flowing into the future, and not a stoppage or a backwash. So it's not surprising that so many mythological saviors are child gods. In the individuation process, the child paves the way for a future change of personality; it anticipates a change of attitude that comes from the synthesis of conscious and unconscious elements in the personality. It is therefore a symbol uniting the opposites. It represents the strongest, the most ineluctable urge in every being, namely the urge to realize itself. It is, as it were, an incarnation of the inability to do otherwise, equipped with all the powers of nature and instinct."

My head swam.

"That's more or less what Jung says, but how might it relate to me?" I asked impatiently.

"I wouldn't know," said Adam, "but I bet you do. J.K. is numinous to you. Something meaningful but unknown always has a fascination for the conscious mind. I can only suggest that you continue to pay attention."

And with that he left me.

I went in the house and pulled Rachel aside from a pile of dough.

"I was talking to Adam about what J.K. might mean to me. He just left me to stew," I complained.

"He abandoned you?"

"He did."

"Poor boy," said Rachel. "The child points to something evolving toward independence. This it cannot do without detaching itself from its origins. Abandonment is therefore a necessary condition of becoming conscious, not just a concomitant symptom."

"You read that somewhere!"

"Higher consciousness, or knowledge going beyond our present-day consciousness, is equivalent to being all alone in the world."

"That's Jung!"

" Good luck."

And she went back to kneading.

I took Sunny down to the beach. With one hand I sifted sand. With the other I leafed through Jung's essay. Sunny sniffed about, eating blades of grass and the tops off flowers.

My mind was going a mile a minute. Thoughts came and went. My eyes fell on this:

> Consciousness hedged about by psychic powers, sustained or threatened or deluded by them, is the age-old experience of mankind. This experience has projected itself into the archetype of the child, which expresses man's wholeness. The "child" is all that is abandoned and exposed and at the same time divinely powerful; the insignificant, dubious beginning, and the triumphal end. The "eternal child" in man is an indescribable experience, an incongruity, a handicap, and a divine prerogative; an imponderable that determines the ultimate worth or worthlessness of a personality.[39]

All told, I was pretty much back to where I'd started. What was moiling about in my unconscious, wanting to surface?

At that point J.K. appeared. "Yo, Daddy-o."

Her hair was dyed purple. She was wearing black leather work-boots, cut-off jeans and a ragged tee-shirt picturing a menagerie

---

[39] Ibid., par. 300.

above the statement: THEY WERE HERE FIRST. On the back of her fire-engine-red knapsack she had carefully lettered:

L♥ve Animals
Don't Eat Them

She clunked herself down beside me and stole one hand into mine. In silence we watched the water.

"Well, my daughter," I finally said, "what do you think? I dreamt I was flying and I've been nesting with bats. I've been talking to myself and now I feel abandoned. Tell me true, has your old man gone bananas?"

She gave me a look and then pulled this drawing out from under her tee-shirt:

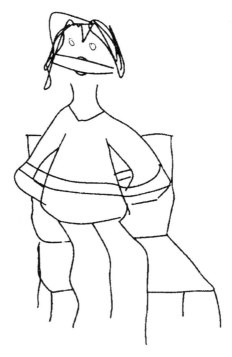

6

The Mana-Personality (1)

I had a good sleep, considering. A raft of dreams, but only one image was notable: Rachel sliding down a pole. I fancied I knew where that came from, but anyway I tucked it into a red file folder labeled FOR AMPLIFICATION. There's usually a lot more to dreams than meets the eye.

After pancakes and bacon garnished with Kiwi fruit and real maple syrup from Quebec—J.K. had Cinnamon Toast Crunch—I returned to an earlier concern.

"Adam," I said. "The other day you spoke of a man who extricates himself from the grip of the collective and thereby saves his soul. He becomes a redeemer, you said, and serves as a beacon of hope for others."

Adam nodded, his back to me. He was standing on a box at the sink, washing the dishes while J.K. dried.

"My question is, what happens to him, the redeemer?"

"Well," said Adam, "according to Jung he becomes a mana-personality, a hero embodying magical or bewitching powers, the *mana* that tribal societies traditionally ascribed to gods or sacred objects."

"And then?"

He rinsed out the sink and thanked J.K. She grabbed a couple of oranges and whizzed out the door, Sunny fast behind.

Adam hopped down and turned to us—Rachel leafing through an art supply catalogue; Norman bent over a crossword; Arnold filing his nails; me with notepad, pencil poised—and scratched his head.

"It is a fine day for canoeing," he said.

That was true; the sun was out and there was no wind at all. The surface of Lake Kagawong was like a mirror. I could do with some exercise. The pants I bought two years ago don't fit; for forty years I was a 32 waist, now 36 is a squeeze.

These thoughts gave me pause. Surely there were better things to do than grapple with theoretical concepts proposed by a man who died over thirty years ago. How did I come to be cooped up in a small damp room, far from my comfortable home, with these mannequins? Manitoulin Island was steeped in history. Why didn't I explore it? I didn't doubt that what I was doing was good, but neither could I lightly dismiss Jung's cautionary remarks about the good being the enemy of the better.[40]

I persisted.

"So what is it about the mana-personality that sets him apart?"

Rachel looked up. "Or her," she corrected.

"One at a time," said Adam, "if you please."

He fussed about, gathering his thoughts and a book or two.

Waiting, I had half a mind to lure Rachel into the bushes—maybe that was the better—but then Adam took over.

"No one acquires mana without first separating from the parents," he began. "Initially, and for many years, the parents are one's closest and most influential relations. There is a symbiotic, mutually dependent connection. Normally, as one grows older, the parental influence is split off: it diminishes in consciousness, but unconsciously the imagos of the parents—the parental complexes—continue to affect attitudes and behavior."

"What generally happens in a man's development is that with increasing age the environmental influence of the parents—and particularly that of the mother—is replaced by a woman, a companion and lover who shares his life and is more or less of the same age. She is not of a superior order, either by virtue of age, authority or physical strength. However, she is a very influential factor and, like the parents, evokes an imago of a relatively autonomous nature, one to which Jung has given the name anima. It is this imago that has magical powers, to wit, mana.

---

[40] "The good is always the enemy of the better. . . . A good thing is unfortunately not a good forever, for otherwise there would be nothing better. If better is to come, good must stand aside." ("The Development of Personality," *The Development of Personality,* CW 17, par. 320)

"With her very dissimilar psychology, woman is and always has been a source of information about things for which a man rarely has eyes. She can inspire him, and her intuitive capacities, often superior to his, can give him timely warning of things to come; her feeling, almost always more personal than his, can show him ways to relate to others that otherwise would not occur to him. All this is doubtless one of the main sources for the historically perceived feminine quality of a man's soul.

"Secondly, apart from the influence of a real live woman, there is the man's own femininity. No man is so entirely masculine that he has nothing womanish about him. It is commonplace in Western culture for a man to carefully guard and hide this fact, to count it as a virtue to repress his feminine traits as much as possible—just as a woman, until relatively recently, considered it unbecoming to be 'mannish'—but behind his masculine façade, often sheer bravado, there is invariably a soft emotional life.

"Naturally, the repression of feminine traits and inclinations causes these contrasexual demands to accumulate in the unconscious. No less naturally, the imago of woman—the soul-image—becomes a receptacle for these demands, which is why a man's love-choice usually corresponds to his own unconscious femininity: in short, a woman who can unhesitatingly receive the projection of his soul. Although such a choice is often regarded and felt as altogether ideal, it may turn out that a man has actually fallen for his own worst weakness. This would explain some highly remarkable pairings."

"And who hasn't known a few," said Norman. He'd lost his heart to many and was now twice divorced.

"The third important source for the femininity of a man's soul," continued Adam, "is the inherited collective image of woman, inborn as a virtual image or psychic aptitude. This inherited image, an accumulation of ancestral experiences, Jung called the anima archetype. It exists in a man's unconscious; it prepares him for women in general and colors the personal nature of his anima complex. The archetype stands behind the complex, as it were, but it's the complex that attracts him to a particular woman."

"I shall never forget Winona," drawled Arnold from the couch.

Winona was Arnold's code-name for any woman who caught his fancy. He knew a good deal about projection, but somehow his relationships never worked out.

"I remember the first time I fell in love," I said. "I was sixteen and it was like being kicked by a horse."

"Do you remember the second time?" asked Adam.

"Yes, I thought I'd been run over by a truck."

"And the third?"—from Rachel.

"Like I'd been poleaxed."

"Fourth?"—Norman.

"A ton of bricks."

I was wracking my brain for more similes—before hooking up with Rachel I had been at the mercy of a flighty anima—when Adam raised his hand.

"You have illustrated the point," he said. "The projection of the anima is not a one-time thing; it's ongoing through life. The corollary, of course, is that the woman it falls upon mirrors the man's psychological state at the time. Perhaps you've heard a Cole Porter song that was popular in my day"—and picking up an egg-beater he warbled into it:

> I've got you under my skin,
> I've got you deep in the heart of me.
> Why should I resist,
> You're really a part of me.
> I've got you under my skin.

"That's it, in more ways than one."

"No offense," said Arnold, "but I prefer Sinatra."

"My favorite was Perry Como," said Norman.

"You guys," said Rachel. "Aretha Franklin is it."

"Please," said Adam.

Well, he started it.

"Now," said Adam, "Jung made the momentous discovery that a compensatory relationship exists between a man's persona and his

anima. Permit me to remind you of some things he says about this."
And he read:

> The persona, the ideal picture of a man as he should be, is inwardly
> compensated by feminine weakness, and as the individual outwardly
> plays the strong man, so he becomes inwardly a woman, i.e., the an-
> ima, for it is the anima that reacts to the persona. But because the
> inner world is dark and invisible to the extraverted consciousness,
> and because a man is all the less capable of conceiving his weak-
> nesses the more he is identified with the persona, the persona's coun-
> terpart, the anima, remains completely in the dark and is at once pro-
> jected, so that our hero comes under the heel of his wife's slipper. If
> this results in a considerable increase of her power, she will acquit
> herself none too well. She becomes inferior, thus providing her hus-
> band with the welcome proof that it is not he, the hero, who is infe-
> rior in private, but his wife. In return the wife can cherish the illu-
> sion, so attractive to many, that at least she has married a hero, un-
> perturbed by her own uselessness. This little game of illusion is of-
> ten taken to be the whole meaning of life.[41]

A reminder, Adam said. Well, I for one had forgotten. If this ever
gets out, I thought, surely fewer relationships would fail.

"The anima," he continued, "is a factor of the utmost importance
in the psychology of a man, especially where his emotions are involved. She intensifies, exaggerates, falsifies and mythologizes all
relations with his work and with other people of both sexes. The resultant fantasies and entanglements are all her doing. When the anima
is strongly constellated, she makes a man moody, jealous, vain and
unadjusted; in a word, he is discontented. Naturally, the man's relationship to the woman who has hooked his anima often accounts for
this, and he is as likely as not to unjustly blame her for it.

"Moreover, in Jung's model of the psyche the character of the
anima can generally be deduced from that of the persona; all those
qualities absent from the outer attitude will be found in the inner.
Jung gives the example of a tyrant tormented by bad dreams and
gloomy forebodings":

---

[41] "Anima and Animus," *Two Essays,* CW 7, par. 309.

Outwardly ruthless, harsh, and unapproachable, he jumps inwardly at every shadow, is at the mercy of every mood, as though he were the feeblest and most impressionable of men. Thus his anima contains all those fallible human qualities his persona lacks.[42]

"Similarly, when a man identifies with his persona, he is in effect possessed by the anima, with all the attendant symptoms."

Identity . . . with the persona automatically leads to an unconscious identity with the anima because, when the ego is not differentiated from the persona, it can have no conscious relation to the unconscious processes. Consequently it *is* these processes, it is identical with them. Anyone who is himself his outward role will infallibly succumb to the inner processes; he will either frustrate his outward role by absolute inner necessity or else reduce it to absurdity, by a process of *enantiodromia*. He can no longer keep to his individual way, and his life runs into one deadlock after another. Moreover, the anima is inevitably projected upon a real object, with which he gets into a relation of almost total dependence.[43]

"You see," said Adam, "how essential it is that a man distinguish between what he is and what he appears to be, both to himself and to others, and also that he should become conscious of the invisible system of relations to his unconscious, especially the anima."

"It's difficult to tell the difference between yourself and something you're unconscious of," observed Norman.

"So it is," nodded Adam. "It is relatively easy for a man to grasp the fact that he and his persona are two different things. But the anima is something else. It takes a great stretch of the conventional mind to acknowledge that one is at the mercy of something invisible. Moreover, when a man recognizes that his ideal persona is responsible for his anything-but-ideal anima, his peace of mind is shattered. The world becomes ambiguous. He is seized by doubts about goodness; worse, he begins to doubt his own good intentions."

"Those are the fellas I like to have in analysis," grinned Arnold.

---

[42] "Definitions," *Psychological Types,* CW 6, par. 804.
[43] Ibid., par. 807.

Me too, I thought; make them aware of their Cretan liar and whoever else is lurking in their wings.

"In the beginning," continued Adam, "the father generally acts as a protection against the dangers of the external world, serving his son as a model persona. Similarly, the mother, as the first bearer of a man's soul-image, his anima, protects him against the dangers that threaten from the dark recesses of his psyche. Primitive puberty rites, though often harsh and uncompromising, dealt with such matters, facilitating the crossover into manhood. Modern man, without such rites, founders."

"We have sporting contests to prove oneself," I noted.

"Gladiatorial affairs," said Adam, "are no substitute for hanging a boy from a tree by a thong through his pectorals."

More than one of us blanched.

"I am far from advocating a return to tribal *rites de passage,*" said Adam, "but the consequence of their lack, in terms of the anima, is that She-Who-Must-Be-Obeyed, in the form of the mother-imago, is transferred to the mate; and the man, as often as not, becomes childish, sentimental, dependent and subservient—or else the exact opposite: truculent, tyrannical, hypersensitive and irrationally protective of what he thinks of as his superior masculinity."

Norman had snuck up on volume 7 and now read:

The safeguard against the unconscious, which is what his mother meant to him, is not replaced by anything in the modern man's education; unconsciously, therefore, his ideal of marriage is so arranged that his wife has to take over the magical role of the mother. Under the cloak of the ideally exclusive marriage he is really seeking his mother's protection, and thus he plays into the hands of his wife's possessive instincts. His fear of the dark incalculable power of the unconscious gives his wife an illegitimate authority over him, and forges such a dangerously close union that the marriage is permanently on the brink of explosion from internal tension.[44]

"Wow!" exclaimed Rachel.

I squeezed her hand.

---

[44] "Anima and Animus," *Two Essays,* CW 7, par. 316.

"In order to deal with this situation," said Adam, "a man must recognize that the world exists inside as well as outside. He must accept that his problems in the outside world stem, at least in part, from difficulties in adapting to the conditions of his inner world."

"Or look for someone else?" suggested Norman.

"Indeed, and find her," nodded Adam, "with the same results."

Norman looked sheepish.

"Take, for example," said Adam, "the spotless man of honor and high morals, public benefactor and defender of the dispossessed, a man whose tantrums and explosive moods terrify his staff, his wife and his children. What is the anima doing here?

"We need only watch what happens as things take their natural course. Wife and children become estranged; a kind of vacuum forms around him. At first he will bewail the hard-heartedness of his family and behave if possible even more vilely than before. That will make the estrangement absolute. If the good spirits have not entirely forsaken him, he will in time notice his isolation and begin to wonder what's behind it: 'What sort of devil has got into me?'—hardly knowing what he says. Then come remorse, reconciliation, oblivion, repression and in next to no time a new explosion.

"In such cases, according to Jung, an irritable anima is trying to enforce a separation; she is like a jealous mistress who would alienate the man from his family. She might even arrange for him to fall in love with someone else, one who promises to ease his troubled soul. But of course the blameless gentleman who is correctly married can be just as correctly divorced, with no fundamental change. The old picture merely receives a new frame. What is required is rather a completely new picture, which is to say a psychological understanding of himself. Until he has sorted himself out, he doesn't know his own mind and therefore can't make a conscious decision about what action to take—if any."

I was intimately acquainted with this pattern. Stripped to the bone, here's what it looks like in a man with a positive mother complex:[45]

---

[45] I cannot speak for men with a negative mother complex, who tend to be

1) He sees promise in a woman's eyes.
2) The reality is disappointing.
3) He blames her for not delivering what she promised.
4) He sees the promise in the eyes of another.
5) Again he's disappointed.
6) Again he blames the woman.

This cycle will repeat itself for as long as the man remains unconscious of his anima and therefore prone to look for her in an actual woman, that is, in projection. Personally, I had followed Jung's advice on how to get quit of it.

First, objectify the anima; refuse to take her moods as your own. Second, face her with the question, "Why do you want such and such?" This recognizes the anima as a separate personality and makes it possible to have a relationship with her. Once you get the knack of dialoguing with your inner woman as an autonomous entity, as someone else, though inextricably linked to your own fate, she can become very helpful. I can tell you she's got me out of many a pickle; I only had to ask.

"From a consideration of the claims of the inner and the outer worlds," Adam was saying, "and from the conflict between them, the possible and the necessary follow. I'm sorry to say that our Western culture—outside of the precepts of alchemy, which is unjustly derided as mystical—has not yet devised a collectively acceptable concept for the union of opposites through the middle path, like the Chinese idea of Tao."

That could have taken us in new directions—and I was not unwilling, having recently agreed to publish a book on the subject[46]—but Rachel preempted me.

"I thought you were going to tell us," she said, "what a man's anima has to do with him becoming a mana-personality."

"Yes," said Adam, "I was about to speak of that—what takes

---

suspicious of women, which I am not. Arnold says the pattern is similar, though for different reasons, but I wouldn't take that as gospel.

[46] See Edward F. Edinger, *The Mystery of the Coniunctio: Alchemical Image of Individuation.*

place psychologically when a man assimilates his anima and thereby takes on her mana."

"Well, I've been wondering," said Rachel, "if maybe there isn't also a *womana*-personality—a woman with charisma? And if so, what's behind that?"

"Something similar, though I think charisma is the wrong word for what we're talking about. Charisma is what we attribute to those in the public eye—entertainers, athletes, industrial magnates and the like—the result of a collective projection onto a persona, behind which may very well be an empty vessel. Of course the same might be said of the traditional notion of *mana,* but nowadays I think the term mana-personality is more appropriately used to describe those who have worked at filling their vessel and as a consequence emanate something special from within."

E-*mana*-te, I noted, being fond of word-play.

"I would be glad to comment on what this looks like in a woman," said Adam, "but I think we needn't coin a new word for it; *mana* is a genderless quality, it can adhere to either sex."

"What about homosexuals and lesbians?" asked Norman.

"There is no reason to think they don't have an inner contrasexual opposite," said Adam. "The fact that it doesn't manifest in the outside world in ways the collective deems normal has more to do with prejudice than with individual psychology."

I would have asked Adam to expand on that, but just then J.K. breezed back in with a pail of minnows and a garter snake, trailed by Sunny with her tongue on the floor.

"Yo, old folks! What's for lunch?"

Adam looked at his watch and patted his stomach.

"Let's eat first," he said to Rachel, "shall we?"

After a meal of home-made lentil soup with fried cheese and onion sandwiches, we regathered by the window looking onto the lake. J.K. had retired to her room and Sunny was flat out under the stairs.

"Women," reminded Rachel.

"Well, I am no expert on female psychology," confessed Adam, "but I know what Jung has to say. Of course I could spin some fancy theories of my own, as many others have, but why would I? Jung knew more than I ever will, and I am entirely satisfied with his model of the psyche—no ifs, ands or buts."

He stuck his little chin out, as if half expecting a fight. Well, he wouldn't get one from me.

"That sounds pretty dogmatic," said Arnold slyly, as if he himself were not.

"Yer darn tootin'," replied Adam. "Slithy toves may gyre and gimble, but I shall not mimsy. By all accounts there is a growing interest in Jungian psychology and I am heartened by that. At the same time, reading what's out there I am struck by the lengths to which Lilliputians will go in their efforts to pinpoint Jung's failings. All in the service of Truth, they say—as if there were such a thing—or to update Jung—as if he weren't far ahead of his time—but I can't help wondering if their unconscious motivation isn't to enhance their own reputations as brilliant thinkers.

"For my part, since my resurrection some forty years ago from misery incarnate, I have taken my stand toe to toe with the Master, seeking only to understand my experience in light of what he wrote. In short, Jung's insights worked for me then and still do. Why should I not trust them? And why else would I?"

"Slavish devotion?" grinned Arnold. "An intransigent father complex?"

"I'd plead no contest to either," declared Adam, "and proud of it."

Norman and Rachel exchanged bemused glances.

"So," said Adam, "we have spoken of a man's anima as a feminine figure that compensates his masculine consciousness. In women, the compensating figure has a masculine character and therefore Jung appropriately termed it the animus."

"Why appropriately?" asked Norman.

"Because *animus* is Latin for spirit, which traditionally, in all cultures everywhere, has been seen as masculine. Of course in some mythologies there are feminine spirits too, and in everyday usage one speaks loosely of a 'feminine spirit,' but Jung was clearly thinking of the *Nous,* the Logos or divine *pneuma*—the Word—principle of logic, structure, judgment and discrimination, which from the beginning of time has been designated as a paternal principle."

"Another case of that consensus thing?" said Norman.

"In effect," nodded Adam.

No one else spoke.

"It is no surprise, then," said Adam, "to find that the unconscious of a woman shows aspects essentially different from those found in a man. Now listen to Jung":

> If I were to attempt to put in a nutshell the difference between man and woman in this respect, i.e., what it is that characterizes the animus as opposed to the anima, I could only say this: as the anima produces *moods,* so the animus produces *opinions;* and as the moods of a man issue from a shadowy background, so the opinions of a woman rest on equally unconscious prior assumptions. Animus opinions very often have the character of solid convictions that are not lightly shaken, or of principles whose validity is seemingly unassailable.[47]

"When these opinions are analyzed," said Adam, "right away we come upon unconscious assumptions whose existence must first be inferred; that is to say, the opinions are conceived *as though* such assumptions existed. In reality the opinions are not thought out at all; they exist ready made, and they are held so positively and with so much conviction that the woman never has the shadow of a doubt about them."

"I didn't," Rachel whispered to me, "until I met you."

I smiled at her.

"Now," continued Adam, "unlike the man's anima, generally the animus does not appear as one person but rather as a plurality, an assembly of fathers or dignitaries of some kind who lay down incontestable *ex cathedra* judgments. But as Jung says":

> On closer examination these exacting judgments turn out to be largely sayings and opinions scraped together more or less uncon-

---

[47] "Anima and Animus," *Two Essays,* CW 7, par. 331.

sciously from childhood on, and compressed into a canon of average truth, justice, and reasonableness, a compendium of preconceptions which, whenever a conscious and competent judgment is lacking (as not infrequently happens), instantly obliges with an opinion. Sometimes these opinions take the form of so-called sound common sense, sometimes they appear as principles which are like a travesty of education: "People have always done it like this," or "Everybody says it is like that."[48]

Norman whistled. "That's quite an indictment."

"Not meant as such, I'm sure," replied Adam. "It is simply a description of what is usual when the animus functions unconsciously, and therefore, just as with the man's anima, negatively. I have known many woman, as Jung certainly did—his wife Emma and soul-mate Toni Wolff come readily to mind—who were not like that, at least not most of the time, and why not? Because they could differentiate between their autonomous opinions and what they really believed. They knew there was a difference.

"And then, of course, you see the other side: a woman well grounded in her personal beliefs and bursting with creative energy— a woman with *mana*. All this is funded, in Jung's model, by a positive animus."

"And dependent on it?" asked Rachel.

Adam adjusted his glasses and peered at her.

"Is her creativity dependent on the masculine?" Rachel repeated.

"Yes," nodded Adam, "that's the implication—but don't mistake this to mean dependence on an actual man. Jung is referring to the contrasexual side of a woman, her inner masculine. The men in her life may come and go. The animus is her constant companion."

"If Jung had used the word tomato for a woman's unconscious masculinity," observed Arnold, "we wouldn't have to have these discussions about semantics."

"Only about vegetables," laughed Rachel.

"In any case," said Adam, "there is an enormous difference between a woman's animus and her male partner, just as there is be-

---

[48] Ibid., par. 332.

tween a man's anima and the woman in his life."

Rachel squeezed *my* hand.

"Now it goes without saying," said Adam, "that the animus is just as often projected as the anima is. So it is not surprising to find that in general a woman's men friends are a mirror image of the state of her animus. If she is unconscious, the men she's attracted to will personify whatever of her world-relating energies are unused or undeveloped. As often as not, they will also be argumentative word-addicts who translate everyday reality into the terminology of the sublime. So it would be insufficient to characterize the animus merely as a conservative, collective conscience; he also has a weakness for intellectual bombast that acts as a pleasant substitute for the onerous task of reflection."

"And he too is a jealous lover," said Rachel knowingly.

"Indeed," said Adam. "When a woman is emotionally involved with a man, her animus is adept at feeding her opinions about him. Unless she has her wits about her, who he is will take second place to her expectations of who he should be.

"You see, animus opinions are invariably collective; they override individual evaluations in exactly the same way as the anima thrusts her emotional poison and projections between a man and the woman in his life. Both alike have bad taste: the anima surrounds herself with inferior feeling, and the animus lets himself be taken in by third-rate thinking.

"A man whose affections are engaged by a woman's physical beauty may, at least initially, find her animus opinions rather child-like and touching, which might lead him to adopt a fatherly or professorial manner. Patronizing, to be sure, but at least benevolent. On the other hand, if the woman does not stir his sentimental side, her opinions will irritate a man to death."

Norman grimaced.

"Men can become incredibly frustrated," said Adam, "when faced with an intransigent animus, as for instance when a woman cornered by male logic proclaims that everyone has a right to an opinion. My own experience is that the animus encourages a critical disputatiousness, which consists essentially in harping on some irrelevant weak point and making it the main one. Or a perfectly lucid discussion gets tangled up in a most maddening way through the introduction of a quite different and perverse point of view. 'Unfortunately, I am always right,' is the attitude of such creatures.

"I don't mean to say that unconscious women deserve their fate at the hands of unconscious men, or vice versa for that matter. Too often the punishment far exceeds the crime. But the inescapable fact is that animus and anima play each other up, so that when they're roused in a given situation, discussion is pointless and anything can happen. Many's the man or woman whose only defense to a charge of assault, or worse, was the feeble plea, 'He wouldn't listen,' or 'I only wanted to teach her a lesson.' "

That silenced us. Random violence in the street was hard enough to live with, without being victimized by your own unconscious.

I was inclined to break it off there. Sunny was growling and digging up the floor. I took that as a plea for fresh air, which frankly I felt the need of myself.

But Adam wasn't quite finished.

"A woman's worst traits in relating to a man," he said, "are due simply to the extraversion of the animus. A woman possessed by the animus is always in danger of losing her femininity, just as an anima-possessed man tends to lack maleness. These psychic changes of sex are due entirely to the fact that a function which belongs inside has been turned outside. This automatically happens when we fail to give adequate recognition to an inner world that is autonomously opposed to the outer, and makes just as serious demands on our capacity for adaptation.

"You see, the animus only interferes with a woman's outside relationships when he is not consciously attended to; his proper function in a woman's psyche is to facilitate her relations with the unconscious—to act as psychopomp or muse—just as the man's anima, when he enters into a real dialogue with her, can be transformed from a nagging virago into a *femme inspiratrice.*"

"So what is one to do?" asked Rachel.

"I can't do better," said Adam, "than read you what Jung says":

The technique of coming to terms with the animus is the same in principle as in the case of the anima; only here the woman must learn to criticize and hold her opinions at a distance; not in order to repress them, but, by investigating their origins, to penetrate more deeply into the background, where she will discover the primordial images, just as the man does in his dealings with the anima. The animus is the deposit, as it were, of all woman's ancestral experiences of man—and not only that, he is also a creative and procreative being, not in the sense of masculine creativity, but in the sense that he brings forth something we might call the . . . spermatic word. Just as a man brings forth his work as a complete creation out of his inner feminine nature, so the inner masculine side of a woman brings forth creative seeds.[49]

"That's the best of life," said Adam. "Then the woman is free; she knows her own task and can relate personally to an outer man, her perceptions unclouded by collective expectations, among which, often enough, is the unconscious belief that the man will save her from herself. He, meanwhile, hero though he'd like to be, has been frantically treading water himself, also hoping to be saved."

"Then who's the savior and who the saved?" I asked.

"Either, both or neither," replied Adam, "It all depends on what happens next."

He cleaned his glasses with a tissue. I rolled a smoke.

"By making animus and anima conscious," said Adam, "we convert them into bridges to the unconscious. So long as they're unconscious, they work their magic as personified complexes, relatively independent personalities who roam about at will, insidiously wrecking relationships. And they can't be integrated into consciousness while their contents remain unknown.

"The purpose of the dialectical process—talking to anima or animus as if they were actual persons—is to become aware of unconscious contents. Only when that's been done, and the conscious mind has become sufficiently familiar with the unconscious pro-

---

[49] Ibid., par. 336.

cesses reflected in their outer manifestations, will they be felt simply as useful psychological functions. Until then"—he flipped over a few pages—"in Jung's graphic words":

> The woman's incubus consists of a host of masculine demons; the man's succubus is a vampire.[50]

Rachel said: "It's really difficult to understand what you're talking about unless you've experienced it."

"Indeed," replied Adam. "But in fact we all have, though not, perhaps, in this light. That's why Jung was more interested in pointing out the ways in which such things are experienced than in presenting a spider's web of intellectual theory. As he noted, all too many learn the words by heart and add the experience in their heads. That doesn't make for change.

"In theory-building, the first things to be discovered are always facts; from the wide-spread discussion of these flow theories that over time are tested, again, against facts. That is the way of science, and if depth psychology is to be anything other than mumbo-jumbo it must submit itself to the same discipline. That's where we come in; at first, perhaps, as aberrant numbers on a graph, but eventually, as our numbers grow, individual experience will become the basis for the graph itself."

Adam started putting books away—it was well past time for his walk, never mind Sunny's.

"But we haven't finished with the mana-personality," I said.

"First things first, my boy. The body has its rhythms. Perhaps we can go on after supper."

Well, we didn't. We played games instead. I could boast that this was a conscious decision, but in fact it just happened. Arnold challenged Norman to a few rounds of Crocinole; I horsed about with Sunny for a bit and then taunted Rachel into a game of Scrabble. The running tally in my head was 443 to 432, for her, and I was keen to catch up.

---

[50] "The Technique of Differentiation," ibid., par. 370.

J.K. spread herself on the floor, surrounded by Adam's magazines on bats that she'd been reading all afternoon.

"Did you know," she said, "that they're more scared than we are when they get trapped? That the ancient Mayans worshipped a bat god? That contrary to popular opinion they don't go for hair? And that the blood of humans is not to their taste at all?"

"Glad to hear it," Norman remarked. "I've always thought those gory stories were sheer projection of our own insatiable blood-lust."

"Play me Battleships next?" pleaded J.K.

Adam, meanwhile, seemed content on his own. He wandered outside to the hammock. And later, looking out the window, I saw him pitching rubber horseshoes with Sunny.

7

The Mana-Personality (2)

"Well, my lovelies, are you open to an excursion?"

It was 8 a.m. Adam was bending over a map of Manitoulin spread on the table. He was wearing pea-green Afghan britches and knee-high leather boots; his Tilley sported a colored plume, like a Swiss mountaineer's hat. Over his shoulder was slung a thick coil of rope.

We gathered around and he pointed out some landmarks.

"South Baymouth, where the ferry lands. Little Current, Sucker Creek, McLean's Mountain Lookout. There's Bridal Veil Falls at Kagawong where the smelt are running. Ice Lake, the airport at Gore Bay. Over here is Meldrum Bay and the Mississagi Lighthouse. Eighty miles, east to west, from Little Current to Meldrum Bay.

"We're here, between Kagawong and West Bay—M'chigeeng in Ojibway, 'Hill of the Fish Harpoon.' There's Whitefish Falls and Dreamer's Rock; according to an Algonquin legend, Kitche Manitou had a vision of the universe that led to its creation. They say that years ago native youths used to climb that rock and dream; there they discovered their guardian spirit and purpose of life—their vocation.

"Here's Sagamuk, Birch Island; it has a long history of native settlement. Early in this century it was the home of Mitigomish, the most powerful medicine man on the North Shore, renowned for his healing powers. There's Great La Cloche Island, and near by is the historic Route of the Voyageurs. That's the waterway used by fur trappers canoeing between Quebec and western Canada some two hundred years ago.

"Ten-Mile Point has a panoramic view of a thousand square miles of North Channel islands; the road past it runs down through Sheguiandah—'Home of the Stork,' there's a museum there—and Batman's Mill, to the First Nation Reserve at Wikwemikong, 'Bay of the Beaver,' where there's an annual summer pow-wow. Dancers

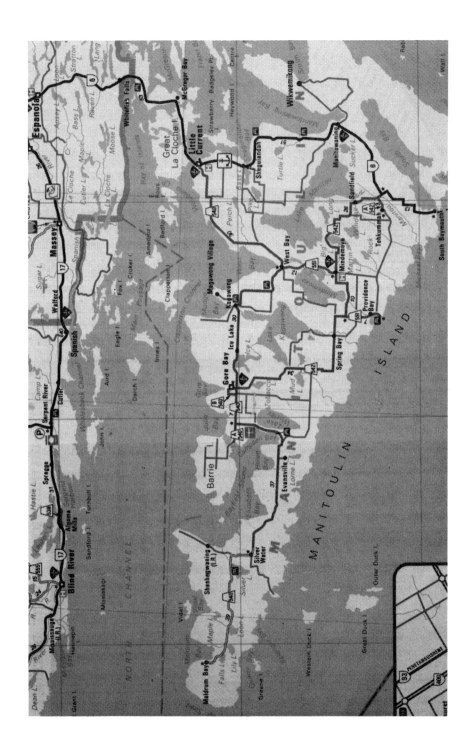

and musicians come from all over North America. Down here is the Ketchankookem Trail . . ."

"Me catchem, you cookem," piped J.K., excited.

". . . and Lake Mindemoya, 'Old Woman,' third largest on Manitoulin, with Treasure Island in the middle. Treasure Island looks like an old woman kneeling. Legend has it that Kitche Manitou sent the hero Nanabozho to teach the Anishnaabeg. Nanabozho was running from the south with his grandmother over his shoulder. She was heavy and when he got to Mindemoya he stumbled. His grandmother flew through the air and landed on her hands and knees in the lake, where she remains to this day.

"Down here is Providence Bay, where there's a mile of sandy beach, and Carter Bay with its famous dunes and crashing waves."

Adam waved at the map.

"In time, Manitoulin might become just another island resort, with time-share condos, a casino and theme park, but now it is unspoiled. Come, what's your pleasure?"

Magical names, so many options.

Arnold said: "Prof, could Manitou/Manitoulin be English corruptions of the native words? I mean, what if Kitche Manitou was originally Kitche *Mana*tou?"

"It is a possibility," smiled Adam.

No one else spoke.

"Well then, I propose a hike up the Cup and Saucer," said Adam brightly, as if that hadn't been his intention from the start. "There's a walk through woods to a cliff overlooking Lake Manitou. It's the island's highest peak, named for its little hill, or cup, sitting on a big hill, the saucer. There's also an adventure trail that I believe will knock your socks off."

"Yay!" cried J.K. "Bears and wolves and woodpeckers!"

Personally I'm partial to elephants, but as that wasn't likely I heard Adam's words with some dread. I'd read a guidebook on his shelf. The dolomite ridge known as the Cup and Saucer is the last leg of the Niagara Escarpment, which starts way down in southern Ontario near Hamilton, runs all the way up to Tobermory, and after

The Cup and Saucer lookout
(from Shelley J. Pearen, *Exploring Manitoulin*)

thirty-four miles under Lake Huron surfaces on Manitoulin. The great attraction of the Cup and Saucer is that after an arduous up-hill climb through a dense forest in which lurk dangerous beasts, you get to enjoy a breathtaking vista from an unprotected lookout that features a drop of 1,150 feet to tree-tops.

Well, my interest in nature walks is minimal, and stairs are climb enough for me. The almost irresistible urge to launch myself into space has tended to keep me away from heights. Just looking at the picture in the book made me dizzy.

However, the others were gung-ho and I was talked into it. While Rachel prepared a picnic lunch I put together a satchel of books. Before long I was beside Adam in the back seat of Rachel's station wagon, with Norman and Arnold scrunched up in the front and J.K. and Sunny in the back compartment.

The Cup and Saucer was about forty minutes away. Adam took the opportunity to bend my ear. I was glad of that, it stopped me from shaking. He picked up yesterday's conversation virtually from where we'd left off.

"Acquiring a mana-personality," said Adam, "is no mean feat. Moreover, it is both a blessing and a curse. The blessing is that you have a better understanding of yourself; the curse is that you become godlike—you know more than others do, and that inevitably leads to inflation and a feeling of isolation."

I nodded. "You are talking about a major change, a transformation of the personality."

"Yes, and fortunately that doesn't happen overnight."

"Fortunately?"

"Because assimilating the activities of anima and animus disrupts life as we have known it. It would drive you crazy—not to mention everyone around you—if it didn't happen over time. Well, I'm sure you know that well enough."

I suppose I should have. I've written a book or two about it. But as a matter of fact I forget what I know from one day to the next. It's as if every morning I have to start from scratch, as if today I'm not who I was yesterday. Maybe that's why I needed these times with Adam—to be reminded.

"All in a day's work," I said.

Adam smiled gently.

"My friend, what drives you?"

This was not an easy question to answer. I have said here earlier that my *raison d'être* was to promote an understanding of Jung's work. That was and is not entirely true. The other side is that I lack the imagination to do anything else, and/or I *am* seeking more laurels; take your pick, I do.

But this wasn't something I wanted to discuss with Adam in the back seat of Rachel's car, so I didn't.

"After the process of differentiation is well entrenched," said Adam, "to the extent that a man no longer identifies with his moods and a woman with her opinions, the contrasexual opposite becomes less personified and autonomous. It is depotentiated, as we say. It no longer exercises demonic power over the ego, and becomes instead a psychological function of relationship between consciousness and the unconscious, a function of an intuitive nature—something like what primitives mean when they say, 'He's gone into the forest to talk with the spirits,' or 'My snake spoke with me,' or, in the mythological language of childhood, 'A little bird told me.' "

"I know a boy like that," exclaimed J.K. "He talks to fish too. And they answer! I mean we're friends and everything but that's really *goofy.*"

"Flora and fauna"—this from Norman—"are the only intelligent life in the universe."

"I used to think fauna was a baby deer," said Arnold.

"Just think of flora as flowers, the plant kingdom," J.K. said, "then fauna is all the birds and animals."

"Animal, vegetable or mineral?" recited Norman. "Say the secret word and win a secret prize!"—the old Groucho Marx radio show. "So what's mineral?"

"Everything else, dummy," said J.K.

"You *said* it! The secret word was 'dummy'!"

"Yay! What's the prize?"

"A week in Jamaica with me—when you're old enough to vote."

This jovial exchange made me think of the way things used to be categorized. Before modern science wrote the rules, people thought the world and everything in it was composed of four elements: air, water, fire and earth. I must say I prefer that model—which incidentally I never heard about in the four years I spent getting a B.Sc.— because it's simpler than the Periodic Table and more in tune with my experience.

Adam was looking through the books I'd packed. He pulled one out and found what he wanted.

"Here's where Jung talks about what happens when anima and animus are no longer autonomous complexes. Listen to this":

Now when the anima loses her mana, what becomes of it? Clearly the man who has mastered the anima acquires her mana, in accordance with the primitive belief that when a man kills the mana-person he assimilates his mana into his own body.

Well then: who is it that has integrated the anima? Obviously the conscious ego, and therefore the ego has taken over the mana. Thus the ego becomes a mana-personality.[51]

"Anna-banana, manima-anima," J.K. cooed to Sunny. "Who is fairest of us all?"

Adam continued reading:

But the mana-personality is a dominant of the collective unconscious, the well-known archetype of the mighty man in the form of hero, chief, magician, medicine-man, saint, the ruler of men and spirits, the friend of God.

This masculine collective figure who now rises out of the dark background and takes possession of the conscious personality entails a psychic danger of a subtle nature, for by inflating the conscious mind it can destroy everything that was gained by coming to terms with the anima. It is therefore of no little practical importance to know that in the hierarchy of the unconscious the anima occupies the lowest rank, only one of many possible figures, and that her subjection constellates another collective figure which now takes over her mana. Actually it is the figure of the magician . . . who attracts the mana to himself . . . . Only in so far as I unconsciously identify with this figure can I imagine that I myself possess the anima's mana. But I will infallibly do so under these circumstances.[52]

"There is an equivalent in a woman," said Adam, "and according to Jung it's no less dangerous. He describes it as 'a sublime, matriarchal figure' "—

The Great Mother, the All-Merciful, who understands everything, forgives everything, who always acts for the best, living only for others, and never seeking her own interests, the discoverer of the great love, just as the magician is the mouthpiece of the ultimate truth. And just as the great love is never appreciated, so the great wisdom is never understood. Neither, of course, can stand the sight of each other.[53]

"Cause for considerable animosity," I observed.

---

[51] "The Mana-Personality," ibid., pars. 376-377.
[52] Ibid., pars. 377-378.
[53] Ibid., par. 379

"You may recall Jung's *bon mots* on that score," said Adam, quoting from his prodigious memory:

> When animus and anima meet, the animus draws his sword of power and the anima ejects her poison of illusion and seduction.[54]

"Mind you," he added, "given the right circumstances—soft lights, romantic music, close dancing and a bit of the grape—they're just as likely to fall in love."

"And thereby hangs many a tale," sighed Norman.

"How do you spell that?" cracked Rachel.

I swear, Sunny wagged hers.

"So," said Adam, "the ego has appropriated something that does not belong to it, and as a result is inflated. But how has it appropriated the mana? If it was really the ego that conquered the contrasexual opposite, then the mana belongs to it and it would be correct to conclude that one has become important. But why doesn't this importance, the mana, work upon others? Surely that would be an essential criterion! Instead, such persons are readily seen by others as being too big for their boots."

We hummed along at fifty miles an hour. I liked the way Rachel drove; she was quick to respond to the unexpected and knew just what the traffic would bear. The road was newly paved and the sun was shining. We had the windows down and the air was heavy with country smells.

"It doesn't work," said Adam, "because in fact one has not become important; one has merely become possessed by an archetype considerably more powerful than anima or animus—the Wise Old Man or the Great Mother. The mistake, you see, is to dream of *victory* over the anima or animus, as opposed to simply coming to terms with the unconscious. When the ego drops its claim to victory, possession by these magical figures automatically ceases."

Arnold turned.

"I went through all that," he said, "and it was no fun. I thought I

---

[54] "The Syzygy: Anima and Animus," *Aion,* CW 9ii, par. 30.

knew everything, and it turned out I knew nothing. Now I leave the knowing to others and just do what comes next."

I remembered. Arnold had lost his friends, his family and his job. All he had left when I met him were his knees. He took heart when he learned that the early Greeks saw the knee as the seat of the soul. Me too; we crawled around the house like a couple of Jose Ferrers playing Toulouse Lautrec.

"You were lucky," said Adam, "you escaped with your life. I'm afraid that many don't. Let me ask you, what do beginning analysts have in common, eh?"

"Poverty," said Arnold. He'd been in debt up to his ears.

"Inflation," corrected Adam. "Having become somewhat less neurotic through their work on themselves, they believe they can heal others, save souls. As a consequence they expect too much, and when they discover that many of those they work with don't change in the slightest, they blame themselves; they aren't good enough, aren't earning their fee and so on. In short, they are failures. That's negative inflation. From having too high an opinion of their abilities, they swing to the other extreme and feel absolutely incompetent—the imposter syndrome, by any other name."

A healthy dose of enantiodromia, I noted. The opposite—or call it a mountain, as René Daumal did,[55] it's that real—is just waiting to give you a spill.

"Of course the truth lies somewhere in the middle," said Adam. "They can only be who they are, and if that doesn't work, too bad. When that realization dawns, if it does, they invariably become better analysts, which is to say more human."

"What about ordinary folk, like me?" asked Norman. He'd had thoughts of becoming an analyst, and even spent some time in Zürich, but it wasn't his fate.

"They're in the same boat," said Adam, "except they don't have to come to grips with it professionally. Anyone who gets this far has to deal with the magnetic pull of the mana-personality. Jung says":

---

[55] See *Mount Analogue*, p. 105.

In differentiating the ego from the archetype of the mana-personality one is now forced, exactly as in the case of the [anima/animus], to make conscious those contents which are specific of the mana-personality. Historically, the mana-personality is always in possession of the secret name, or of some esoteric knowledge, or has the prerogative of a special way of acting . . . in a word, it has an individual distinction. Conscious realization of the contents composing it means, for the man, the second and real liberation from the father, and, for the woman, the liberation from the mother, and with this comes the first genuine sense of his or her true individuality.[56]

"Then what happens to the mana?" I asked.

"Good question," said Adam. "Jung did puzzle over that. Who or what, he wondered, becomes mana when even the magician can no longer work magic? . . ."

"Look!" cried J.K., "deer!"

There they were, a few hundred feet ahead, grazing by the side of the road. Rachel slowed to a crawl. Two magnificent creatures. They shied as we got closer and sprang with great graceful leaps back into the bush.

"Cool," murmured J.K.

"A propitious event," declared Adam, with some excitement, "not to say synchronistic. The stag is well-known as a symbol of the soul, and the unicorn represents spirit. Together, and embodied, they are the key to what the alchemists called the *coniunctio*—the coming together of the opposites, the goal of individuation."

"I dunno," said Arnold. "I didn't see any unicorn."

"I did," said J.K. "There was one with antlers and the other had a horn, I'm sure!"

"I was driving," said Rachel.

"I was watching their feet," said Norman. "Did you notice how they splayed when they pranced?"

Arnold jabbed him.

"They didn't prance, they stood—dumb as a tree!"

"What's so dumb about a tree?" asked J.K.

---

[56] "The Mana-Personality," *Two Essays,* par. 393.

Adam said, with unusual gravity: "I believe we have been blessed by the gods."

J.K., temperamentally practical but still of an age when anything is possible—and, like Arnold, a Leo, afraid of nothing—hung her chin on the back of the seat between Adam and me.

"What do they look like, these gods?"

"They have fangs," said Adam.

J.K. made a face and sank back. I shrugged her a smile and brought Adam back to my question.

"So what happens to the mana?"

Adam reflected.

"To be honest, nobody knows for sure. But Jung surmised that when the ego drops all pretense to victory over the unconscious, there is established a balance of power between the two worlds.

"Here's what he says":

> The dissolution of the anima [or animus] means that we have gained insight into the driving forces of the unconscious, but not that we have made these forces ineffective. They can attack us at any time in new form. And they will infallibly do so if the conscious attitude has a flaw in it. It's a question of might against might. If the ego presumes to wield power over the unconscious, the unconscious reacts with a subtle attack, deploying the dominant of the mana-personality, whose enormous prestige casts a spell over the ego. Against this the only defence is full confession of one's weakness in face of the powers of the unconscious. By opposing no force to the unconscious we do not provoke it to attack.[57]

Again I asked: "And what happens to the mana?"

"Well, Jung believes it accrues to something that is both conscious and unconscious, or else neither—a mid-point of the personality, an ineffable something between the opposites which in effect unites them. Jung saw this as a profoundly important step forward on the journey of individuation."

"The mid-point . . ." I said, "the transcendent function?"

"Yes. When every motive of will has an equally strong counter-

---

[57] Ibid., par. 391.

motive—which is to say, when the conflict between consciousness and the unconscious is at its peak—there is a damming up of vital energy. But life can't tolerate a standstill. If the ego can hold the tension, something quite unexpected happens: a *third* manifests—a new attitude toward oneself and the world. The tendencies of conscious and unconscious are the two factors that together make up the transcendent function. Jung called it transcendent because it makes the transition from one attitude to another organically possible.

"As a matter of fact, this progression is analogous to the ancient alchemical precept known as the Axiom of Maria: 'One becomes two, two becomes three, and out of the third comes the one as the fourth.'[58] This cogent observation underpinned the alchemical *opus* for centuries, though it never made it, alas, into modern textbooks of chemistry."

Norman turned his head. "A woman alchemist?"

"Yes," said Adam. "Of course in the literature, written by men, they mostly figure as assistants, the alchemist's *soror mystica*—his anima, we would say—but I don't doubt there were many women who took the lead. Maria Prophetissa was only the most famous. Jung saw her dictum as a metaphor for the whole process of individuation, and I'm not surprised. Think of it like this: *One* stands for the original, paradisical state of unconscious wholeness; *two* signifies the conflict between opposites; *three* points to a potential resolution; *the third* is the transcendent function; and *the one as the fourth* is alchemical code for the Philosophers' Stone—psychologically equivalent to a transformed state of conscious wholeness.

"It's a kind of circular odyssey, you see, a uroboric journey, where the aim is to get back to where you started, only in the end you know where you've been."

"How much longer to Cuppan Saucer?" asked J.K.

I suspected Sunny was getting restless too; she kept hurling herself against the window.

Norman, who had the map, said, "Just ahead."

---

[58] See *Psychology and Alchemy*, CW 12, par. 26.

"So now," Adam went on, "with this new attitude, you'd think a person would be out of the woods, right? Safe and secure, whole and happily ever after?"

"Not!" cried J.-K.

Adam stilled her with a glance.

"In fact, though no longer easy prey for anima/animus devils, and wary of the mana-personality, you've only weathered the first stage of an ongoing initiation. Listen to Jung":

> This part of the process corresponds exactly to the aim of the con-cretistic primitive initiations up to and including baptism, namely, severance from the "carnal" (or animal) parents, and rebirth *in novam infantiam,* into a condition of immortality and spiritual childhood, as formulated by certain mystery religions of the ancient world, among them Christianity.[59]

"Here we are," announced Rachel, pulling into a small parking lot beside a log-cabin café, the Coldsprings Outpost. There were a few other cars and people milling about. Beside an entrance some hundred feet away a big wooden sign proclaimed:

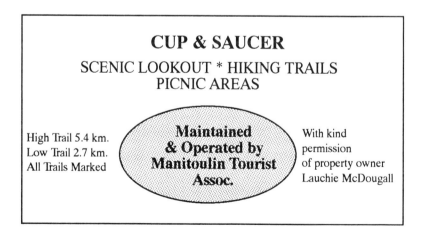

CUP & SAUCER
SCENIC LOOKOUT * HIKING TRAILS
PICNIC AREAS

High Trail 5.4 km.
Low Trail 2.7 km.
All Trails Marked

Maintained & Operated by Manitoulin Tourist Assoc.

With kind
permission
of property owner
Lauchie McDougall

Well, I would like to say I skipped fearlessly into the forest—as J.K. and Sunny immediately did—and after a fascinating stroll to the

---

59 "The Mana-Personality," *Two Essays,* par. 393.

lookout had a jolly old time dangling my feet over the drop. But I chickened out. The others cajoled and Adam offered his rope.

"Come now, we'll tie it from you to a tree."

"No thanks," I said, "I don't know where it's been."

I waved them away and for the next two hours curled up in a corner of the Outpost with my pack of books. I was intrigued by what Adam had said and read, and more interested in what happened next inside than in any panoramic outer view.

In *Two Essays* I found this:

> It is now quite possible that, instead of identifying with the mana-personality, one will concretize it as an extramundane "Father in Heaven," complete with the attribute of absoluteness—something that many people seem very prone to do. This would be tantamount to giving the unconscious a supremacy that was just as absolute . . . so that all value would flow over to that side. The logical result is that the only thing left behind here is a miserable, inferior, worthless, and sinful little heap of humanity.[60]

There was a footnote:

> "Absolute" means "cut off," "detached." To assert that God is absolute amounts to placing him outside all connection with mankind. Man cannot affect him, or he man.[61]

Well, Jung certainly couldn't buy that. In "Answer to Job" he claims God needs man in order to become conscious of how unconscious He is.[62] I mean that was really tempting fate. Does the fact that Jung wasn't struck by lightning or a dose of boils mean there is no God? Was Nietzsche right after all? Maybe He just wasn't listening, or laughing too hard to answer, or too busy raising the sun. Arnold says anything's possible if you aren't afraid to speculate.

Anyway, Jung warns against mistaking the archetype of the mana-personality for God:

---

[60] Ibid., par. 394.

[61] Ibid., note 6.

[62] *Psychology and Religion,* CW 11, pars. 553ff; see also Edward F. Edinger, *Transformation of the God-Image: An Elucidation of Jung's* Answer to Job.

He must not be concretized, for only thus can I avoid projecting my values and non-values into God and Devil, and only thus can I preserve my human dignity, my specific gravity, which I need so much if I am not to become the unresisting shuttlecock of unconscious forces.[63]

Now that metaphor really hit home. As a teen-ager, when I wasn't fishing or playing pool or reading science-fiction, I was trying to make my mark on a badminton court.

I read on:

We stand with our soul suspended between formidable influences from within and without, and somehow we must be fair to both. This we can do only after the measure of our individual capacities. Hence we must bethink ourselves not so much of what we "ought" to do as of what we *can* and *must* do.

Thus the dissolution of the mana-personality through conscious assimilation of its contents leads us, by a natural route, back to ourselves as an actual, living something, poised between two world-pictures and their darkly discerned potencies. This "something" is strange to us and yet so near, wholly ourselves and yet unknowable, a virtual centre of so mysterious a constitution that it can claim anything—kinship with beasts and gods, with crystals and with stars— without moving us to wonder, without even exciting our disapprobation.[64]

Oh, I wish he hadn't said crystals. That's bound to be picked up by New Agers. But at least he makes it clear that his intention is neither to deify man nor to dethrone God. Jung does favor a psychological God, one that isn't projected and that moreover functions as a regulating center of the psyche.

Here's what I pieced together:

I have called this centre the *self.* Intellectually the self is no more than a psychological concept, a construct that serves to express an unknowable essence which we cannot grasp as such, since by definition it transcends our powers of comprehension. It might equally well be called the "God within us." . . .

---

[63] "The Mana-Personality," *Two Essays,* par. 395
[64] Ibid., pars. 397-398.

When, therefore, we make use of the concept of a God we are simply formulating a definite psychological fact, namely the independence and sovereignty of certain psychic contents which express themselves by their power to thwart our will, to obsess our consciousness and to influence our moods and actions.

The conception of God as an autonomous psychic content makes God into a moral problem—and that, admittedly, is very uncomfortable. But if this problem does not exist, God is not real, for nowhere can he touch our lives. He is then either an historical and intellectual bogey or a philosophical sentimentality.

If we leave the idea of "divinity" quite out of account and speak only of "autonomous contents," we maintain a position that is intellectually and empirically correct, but we silence a note which, psychologically, should not be missing. By using the concept of a divine being we give apt expression to the peculiar way in which we experience the workings of these autonomous contents. We could also use the term "daemonic," provided that this does not imply that we are still holding up our sleeves some concretized God who conforms exactly to our wishes and ideas. . . . Therefore, by affixing the attribute "divine" to the workings of autonomous contents, we are admitting their relatively superior force. And it is this superior force which has at all times constrained men to ponder the inconceivable, and even to impose the greatest sufferings upon themselves in order to give these workings their due. It is a force as real as hunger and the fear of death.

The self could be characterized as a kind of compensation of the conflict between inside and outside. . . . [It] has somewhat the character of a result, of a goal attained, something that has come to pass very gradually and is experienced with much travail. So too the self is our life's goal, for it is the completest expression of that fateful combination we call individuality, the full flowering not only of the single individual, but of the group, in which each adds his portion to the whole.

Sensing the self as something irrational, as an indefinable existent, to which the ego is neither opposed nor subjected, but merely attached, and about which it revolves very much as the earth revolves round the sun—thus we come to the goal of individuation.[65]

---

[65] Ibid., pars. 399f.

I think I got it. If you can depotentiate your complexes and then take on God as a personal moral problem instead of an omnipotent being "out there," and if you acknowledge that after all you're back to square one, why then you have your hands full and don't have to worry about the mana-personality.

It was warm in the Outpost. I dozed off and dreamt all my teeth fell out. I woke up with J.K. bouncing in my lap.

"Dad! I squoze through a rock chimney! I crawled along a ledge no wider'n me! I was scared but I did it!"

Was this it, I thought, my new life? Bad grammar and all? Was this child real, or did I imagine her? Or was she, perhaps, imagined by something in me?

"Squeezed, please," I said, hugging her.

8

The Christ Model

"Adam," I said. "I have been struggling to understand Jung's use of Christ as an example of personality."

It was the morning of our last day on Manitoulin. Norman was going to stay on for a few days, but the rest of us were packed for a run to the five o'clock ferry.

Adam and I were on the deck, Sunny at our feet. The others had gone to a country auction at Maple Point, where Rachel hoped to find a dresser. J.K. was looking for camping gear and a life-jacket; next week she was going canoeing with her class in Algonquin Park. Arnold and Norman went along for the ride.

The sky was cloudless, the air warm. The black flies had debouched for the season and it was still too early for mosquitoes, who according to Adam are programmed to arrive in mid-June.

He looked at the lake and set about filling his pipe.

"Of course in other religions there are figures that are quite as exemplary," he said. "Jung certainly knew them. I believe he focused on Christ because of his own background—he was a preacher's son, after all—and because the example of Christ was more accessible to Western readers. However many unbelievers there are, Christ is still the dominant myth of our culture."

I looked at my notes.

"Jung's exact words are: 'One of the most shining examples of the meaning of personality that history has preserved for us is the life of Christ.' "[66]

"That's certainly in line with what we've been talking about," said Adam. "Think of the historical context. In Christianity, which incidentally was the only religion really persecuted by the Romans, there

---

[66] "The Development of Personality," *The Development of Personality,* CW 17, par. 309.

arose a direct opponent of the Caesarian madness that afflicted not only the emperor but every Roman as well. The opposition showed itself wherever the worship of Caesar clashed with Christianity. This was personified by the man Jesus; he offered salvation from the current hell on earth. In the beginning he was a hero; in the end he was a scapegoat for the enantiodromian shift in the Zeitgeist. He was no impostor either, no clay-footed word-monger; he wrestled in himself with the opposites that were tearing his country apart."

He stood up. "Just a minute."

He went inside and came out with a couple of books. One was volume 17 of the Collected Works, which he opened at Jung's well-thumbed essay on personality.

"Listen to this," he said:

> As we know from what the evangelists tell us about the psychic development of Christ's personality, this opposition [between God and Caesar] was fought out just as decisively in the soul of [Christ]. The story of the Temptation clearly reveals the nature of the psychic power with which Jesus came into collision: it was the power-intoxicated devil of the prevailing Caesarean psychology that led him into dire temptation in the wilderness. This devil was the objective psyche that held all the peoples of the Roman Empire under its sway, and that is why it promised Jesus all the kingdoms of the earth, as if it were trying to make a Caesar of him.[67]

"But Jesus knew what he had to do and stood firm," said Adam. "Obeying the inner call of his vocation, he voluntarily exposed himself to the assaults of the imperialistic madness that filled everyone, conqueror and conquered alike. In this way he recognized the nature of the objective psyche that had plunged the whole world into misery and had begotten a yearning for salvation that found expression even in the pagan poets. Far from suppressing or allowing himself to be suppressed by this psychic onslaught, Jesus let it act on him consciously and he assimilated it. Thus was world-conquering Caesarism transformed into spiritual kingship, and the Roman Empire into the universal kingdom of God that was not of this world."

---

[67] Ibid.

I was beginning to get the picture. I'd read Jung's words myself with little comprehension. Once again I was amazed at how their meaning became clearer when relayed by Adam. Brilligant, indeed.

"Jesus pointed out to humanity the old truth," he said, "that where force rules there is no love, and where love reigns force does not count. The religion of love was the exact psychological counterpart to the Roman devil-worship of power. Christianity was thus the timely compensation for Caesarism, and Christ was its standard-bearer, ergo a hero. His unique life has become a sacred symbol because it is the psychological prototype of the only meaningful life, one that strives for the individual realization, absolute and unconditional, of its own particular law.

"And that, of course, is the challenge of personality. Whoever doesn't rise to this challenge, whoever is untrue to the law of his or her own being, has failed to realize the meaning of their life."

That sounded pretty harsh to me—I mean it left so many out—but I resolved to reflect on it.

"The ideal of personality," said Adam, "is an ineradicable need of the human soul; failing its realization in oneself, it will be projected onto someone or something else—self-professed saviors of whatever stamp, and isms that in a wink would plunge us into war, as they have countless times in the past.

"Here's what Jung wrote in the early thirties, and I think it's quite as relevant today":

> The deification of Jesus, as also of the Buddha, is not surprising, for it affords a striking example of the enormous valuation that humanity places upon these hero figures and hence upon the ideal of personality. Though it seems at present as if the blind and destructive dominance of meaningless collective forces would thrust the ideal of personality into the background, yet this is only a passing revolt against the dead weight of history. Once the revolutionary, unhistorical, and therefore uneducated inclinations of the rising generation have had their fill of tearing down tradition, new heroes will be sought and found.[68]

---

68 Ibid., par. 311.

"What do you think it was in people," I asked, "that was stirred by the Christian message?"

"That's a psychological question," said Adam. "To answer it we'd have to examine the Christ symbolism contained in the New Testament, together with the patristic allegories and medieval iconography, and then compare that material with the archetypal content of the unconscious psyche in order to determine what archetypes had been constellated."

"Cripes," I said, feeling like a Dummling, "that's a tall order."

"Well," said Adam, "the most important of the symbolical statements about Christ are those that reveal the attributes of the hero's life: improbable origin, divine father, hazardous birth, rescue in the nick of time, precocious development, conquest of the mother and of death, miraculous deeds, a tragic early end, signs and marvels after death and so on. As the Logos, Son of the Father, Redeemer and Savior, Christ is himself God, an all-embracing totality. As a shepherd he is the leader and center of the flock. He is the vine and those that hang on him are the branches. . . ."

"His body bread to be eaten, his blood wine to be drunk," I recalled the litany.

". . . the hero and the God-man," nodded Adam, "born without sin, more complete and more perfect than the natural man, who is to him what a child is to an adult, or an animal to a human being.

"Now, these mythological statements, coming both from within the Christian sphere and from outside it, are descriptive of an archetype that expresses itself in essentially the same symbolism. It also occurs in individual dreams or in fantasy projections onto living people, as in hero-worship. The content of all such symbolic products is the idea of an overpowering, all-embracing, complete or perfect being, represented either by a person of heroic proportions or by an animal with magical attributes, or sometimes by a magic vessel or some other 'treasure hard to attain' such as a jewel, ring or crown. This archetypal idea is a reflection of the individual's wholeness, that is, of the Self, present in everyone as an unconscious image.

"I believe it was this archetype of the Self in the individual soul that responded to the Christian message, with the result that the human Rabbi Jesus was quickly assimilated by the constellated archetype. In this way Christ realized the idea of the Self. But as one can never distinguish empirically between a symbol of the Self and a God-image, the two ideas always appear blended together. Psychologically speaking, the domain of the gods begins where consciousness leaves off. To the symbols of wholeness that come to us from there—the collective unconscious—we attach names that vary according to time and place."

"So that's why Jung also considered Christ to be a symbol of the Self?" I asked, thinking of his long discourse in *Aion.*[69]

"Indeed," said Adam, "though there are some caveats. Jung defined the Self as the psychic totality of the individual, so anything one might postulate as being a greater totality than oneself can become a symbol of the Self. For this reason any particular Self-symbol is seldom as total as the definition would require. Even the Christ-figure is not a totality, for it lacks the nocturnal side of the psyche, the darkness of the spirit, and is also without sin. Without the integration of evil there is no genuine totality."

I took the point, but the discussion was becoming rather too abstract for me. Too grand-scale, maybe, for my mundane temperament. So I pressed Adam to comment on the therapeutic application of what we'd been discussing these past few days.

"In the first place," said Adam, "we must be mindful of the personality of the analyst as a curative or harmful factor. That's why Jung insisted that anyone intending to practice psychotherapy should at the very least become acquainted with the effects of the unconscious on his or her own person, and to this end undergo a thorough training analysis—the self-education of the educator, you see. Everything required of the patient on an objective level—confession, elucidation, education and so forth—must first be experienced subjectively by the analyst. That is to say, the doctor can no longer hide behind the *persona medici,* evading his own problems by treating

---

[69] See "Christ, A Symbol of the Self," *Aion,* CW 9ii.

those of others. The man who suffers from a running abscess is not fit to perform a surgical operation."

What a great line, I thought; I shall tell Rachel.

"Just as the momentous discovery of an unconscious shadow-side in man forced the Freudian school to deal even with the questions of religion," said Adam, "so the self-education of the analyst turns the spotlight on one's ethical attitude. The self-criticism and self-examination that are indissolubly bound up with it necessitate a view of the psyche radically different from the merely biological one that used to prevail. It turns out that the human psyche is far more than an object of scientific interest; it is not only the sufferer but the doctor as well, not only the object but also the subject, not only a cerebral function but the absolute condition of consciousness itself.

"And, as an added bonus, as soon as psychotherapy included the doctor as its subject, it transcended its medical origins and ceased to be merely a method for treating the sick. It burst the bonds that had confined it to the consulting room. Thus the process of analysis became just as valuable for the healthy, whose sickness is at most the suffering that torments us all."

Adam paused to relight his pipe.

"Moreover," he continued, "we now know that there is a demonstrable compensatory relationship between personality and neurosis: the more highly developed the personality—that is, differentiated—the fewer the neurotic symptoms; and the more archaic the personality—which is to say unconscious—the more neurotic.

"Neurosis, after all, is essentially a developmental disturbance. It bespeaks a deviation, one way or another, from one's proper path. Therefore analysts, as physicians of the soul, are compelled by professional necessity to concern themselves with the problem of personality and the inner voice.

"Here's how Jung put it":

Neurosis is . . . a defence against the objective, inner activity of the psyche, or an attempt, somewhat dearly paid for, to escape from the inner voice and hence from the vocation. . . . Behind [neurosis] is concealed [one's] vocation, [one's] destiny: the growth of personality, the full realization of the life-will that is born with the individual. It is the man without *amor fati* who is the neurotic; he, truly, has missed his vocation.

In practical psychotherapy these psychic facts, which are usually so vague and have so often degenerated into empty phrases, emerge from obscurity and take visible shape. Nevertheless, it is extremely rare for this to happen spontaneously as it did with Old Testament prophets; generally the psychic conditions that have caused the [neurotic] disturbance have to be made conscious with considerable effort. But the contents that then come to light are wholly in accord with the inner voice and point to a predestined vocation, which, if accepted and assimilated by the conscious mind, conduces to the development of personality.[70]

"Just as the great personality acts upon society to liberate, to transform and to heal," said Adam, "so the birth of personality in oneself has a therapeutic effect. It is as if a river that had run to waste in sluggish side-streams and marshes suddenly found its way back to its proper bed, or as if a stone lying on a germinating seed were lifted away so that the shoot could begin its natural growth."

Oh boy. I was off and flying, transported by the power of metaphor. Adam brought me back to earth.

"What is the central image of the Christian myth?" he snapped.

Instantly I was back in Sunday school, the basement of a United Church, where Miss Peters would rap my knuckles with a ruler when I went blank. I learned to recite the names of all the Books in the New Testament, backward even.

I shook my head. This was Adam and I wasn't in a basement.

"Umm . . . the virgin birth?"

"The crucifixion. And what is the prime symptom of neurosis?"

That was easier. "Conflict."

"Yes. For almost two thousand years," said Adam, "the image of a man nailed to a cross has been the supreme symbol of Western civilization. And why is that? Because it is such a graphic image of

---

[70] "The Development of Personality," *The Development of Personality,* CW 17, pars. 313, 316.

conflict—being torn between the opposites."

He picked up the other book he had brought out. It was one I had written myself. The cover was a drawing by Franz Kafka showing a man tied to poles that could tear tear him apart .

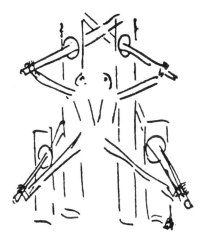

Then, and to my great pleasure, Adam read out a passage I had all but forgotten writing some fifteen years ago:

> The tension involved in the conflict between ego and shadow is commonly experienced as a kind of crucifixion. This symbolizes the suffering involved in differentiating the opposites and learning to live with them. Writes Jung:
>
> "Nobody who finds himself on the road to wholeness can escape that characteristic suspension which is the meaning of crucifixion. For he will infallibly run into things that thwart and "cross" him: first, the thing he has no wish to be (the shadow); second, the thing he is not (the "other," the individual reality of the "You"); and third, his psychic non-ego (the collective unconscious)."[71]

Brillig quoting me quoting Jung. I did like being in the middle.

"You had the right idea," said Adam. "Conflict heralds the birth of consciousness. Remember the Axiom of Maria?—*One becomes two.*

---

[71] *The Secret Raven: Conflict and Transformation,* p. 40. The Jung passage is from "The Psychology of the Transference," *The Practice of Psychotherapy,* CW 16, par. 470.

The blissful state of unconscious wholeness is forever sundered by the awareness of opposites. Christ's struggle between good and evil is the tip of a massive iceberg, and just as the Crucifixion was the culmination of his earthly life, so its psychological equivalent, conflict, is the beginning of individuation. The Resurrection, then, is psychologically analogous to rebirth: what one was has died; long live the new you."

Sunny suddenly stood and sniffed the air, ears and tail erect. She vaulted off the deck and into the woods. A squirrel or badger, a woodchuck? I wished I could see what she could smell. Sure, Sunny hides from thunder, as I do from heights, but I'm the one who chases chimeras.

"There's another way to think of the Christ model," Adam was saying. "The goal of psychological, as of biological, development is self-realization—individuation. But since we know ourselves only as an ego, and since the Self is indistinguishable from a God-image, then self-realization, in religious or metaphysical terms, amounts to God's incarnation. That is already expressed in the fact that Christ is the son of God. And because individuation is an heroic and often tragic task, the most difficult of all, it invariably involves suffering, a passion of the ego: the ordinary, empirical person we once were is burdened with the fate of becoming lost in a greater dimension and so being robbed of a fancied freedom of will. And thus we suffer, strange as this may sound, from the violence done to us by the Self. The analogous passion of Christ signifies God's suffering on account of the injustice of the world and the darkness of man.

"Do you see? The human and the divine suffering set up a relationship of complementarity with compensating effects. Through the Christ-symbol, we can get to know the real meaning of our suffering on the way toward realizing our wholeness. As a result of the integration of conscious and unconscious, one's ego enters the divine realm, where it participates in God's suffering. The cause of the suffering is in both cases the same, namely incarnation, which on the human level appears as individuation."

That was considerably more than I had a mind for at ten o'clock in the morning. Still, I wrote it down, and as I did so out popped a question.

"Adam, do you really think that following the inner voice leads to a fuller life, a more comprehensive consciousness?"

He settled back and eyed me.

My face reddened. I felt like an apostate, a Doubting Thomas who would unaccountably let the side down. To tell the truth—well, as far as that's possible—it was more the kind of remark that would come from Arnold. All the same, I had to own it.

"Yes," said Adam simply. "Why do you think mythological accounts of the birth of the hero or a symbolic rebirth coincide with sunrise? I'll tell you: because the growth of personality is synonomous with an increase of light, which is to say consciousness."

My mind flashed back to Adam's ritual morning offering of spit to the sun. Still, I had some difficulty with what he was saying, for among my inner voices there were some that were quite dark.

"What if you don't like the voice you hear?" I asked. "What if it says awful things?"

"My boy, count your lucky stars you hear it at all. What we don't hear will get us from behind, drive us inexorably to act out its will. As a matter of fact the inner voice is generally something negative, if not downright evil. Why? Think about it in terms of the self-regulation of the psyche. It must be so because first of all we are not as conscious of our vices as we are of our virtues, and secondly, because we suffer less from the good than from the bad in us. Whenever we get too far out on a limb, which like as not is our best foot hovering in space, the psyche attempts to balance the scales—accidents, depression, anxiety, conflict and so on. Of course nothing will change unless the ego takes such symptoms to heart.

"If need be, and especially to compensate a high-and-mighty conscious attitude, the inner voice will be a dyed-in-the-wool Lucifer who presents evil in a very seductive and convincing way, in order to make us succumb. That is the psychological basis for Christ's temptation in the wilderness, and incidentally my own experience on the Niederdorf. This Luciferian voice typically faces us with difficult moral decisions; only in the process of grappling with these can we achieve personality.

"Of course we must succumb a little, if only to come to grips with our devilish contents. Recall the psychological rule: 'When an inner situation is not made conscious, it happens outside, as fate.' "[72]

Sunny was back, licking her chops. Nature red in tooth and claw.

"On a collective level," said Adam, "so long as most people are undivided, unconscious of their inner opposite, the world itself will act out the conflict and be torn into opposing halves."

Now that was a sobering thought. The Cold War between East and West was ostensibly over, but still the opposites took their toll in smaller enclaves.

I rolled another cigarette.

"The Christ-image is a powerful metaphor," I said, "but how can anyone live up to that? It's as good as perfect."

"Yes," agreed Adam, "or at least meant to be. Although Jung upheld the course of Christ's life as a model for the process of individuation, he also pointed out that the Christian myth has done a great disservice to the feminine. Nor should we forget the difference between perfection and completeness. Human beings may strive after perfection, but we invariably suffer from the opposite of our intentions for the sake of completeness. As the Bible says, 'When I would do good, evil is present with me.' "[73]

Adam became very serious then, as if a cloud had crossed the sun. He clasped his hands and leaned forward.

"I trust you realize it is dangerous to touch on these issues. There are times in the world's history, and our own may be one, when good must give way for something that is better. But evil so easily slips in on the plea that it is, at least potentially, the better. We must forever keep alert. Listening to the inner voice is full of pitfalls and hidden snares. The highest and the lowest, the best and the vilest, the truest and the most deceptive things are often blended together in the

---

[72] "Christ, A Symbol of the Self," *Aion,* CW 9ii, par. 126.
[73] Rom. 7: 21, Authorized Version.

most baffling way, thus opening up in us an abyss of confusion,
falsehood and despair."

I wrote furiously to keep up.

"It is treacherous, slippery ground," said Adam, "this question of
what is right and what is wrong, as dangerous and pathless as life
itself when one lets go of the railings."

He picked up volume 17 and read:

He who cannot lose his life, neither shall he save it. The hero's birth
and the heroic life are always threatened. The serpents sent by Hera
to destroy the infant Hercules, the python that tries to strangle
Apollo at birth, the massacre of the innocents, all these tell the same
story. To develop the personality is a gamble, and the tragedy is that
the daemon of the inner voice is at once our greatest danger and an
indispensable help. It is tragic, but logical, for it is the nature of
things to be so.[74]

"The truth as I know it," said Adam, "is that the process of individuation, when it befalls a person, may lead to salvation or calam-
ity. As long as one is contained within a church or religious creed,
one is spared the dangers of direct experience. But whoever falls out
of containment in a religious myth, and nowadays they are many, is
a prime candidate for individuation.

"Jesus became the tutelary image or amulet against the archetypal
powers that threatened to possess the people of his time. Similar
powers besiege us today. But it is not a slavish imitation of Christ
that is called for. No sir! Rather we must assimilate what the Christ-
image means in terms of a life well and truly lived according to the
soulful dictates of the individual heart.

"In the end, the hero, the leader, the savior, is one who discovers
a new way to greater certainty. Everything could be left undisturbed
did not the new way demand to be discovered, and did it not visit us
with all the plagues of Egypt until it finally is known. The undiscov-
ered vein within us is a living part of the psyche; classical Chinese
philosophy names this interior way Tao, and likens it to a flow of

---

[74] "The Development of Personality," *The Development of Personality,* CW
17, par. 321.

water that moves irresistibly toward its goal. To find Tao means fulfillment, wholeness, one's destination reached, one's mission done—the beginning, end and perfect realization of the meaning of one's existence. Personality is Tao."

Adam's pipe was out again. He emptied the ashes over the side of the deck and set about refilling it. He spoke calmly now.

"There will always be those who aren't satisfied with the mores of collective life. Some are moral renegades who abide no restraint. Let the law of the land deal with them, and good riddance. Others, who have heard the call to an individual life, are the chosen ones. Under cover and by devious paths they set forth to their destruction or salvation, seeking direct experience of the eternal roots. Following the lure of the restless objective psyche, they find themselves alone in the wilderness. Will they save their souls, become personalities? Will they individuate? Discover who they are, really?"

He looked directly at me, head slightly cocked, half a smile on his gnomish face. "Will you?"

I didn't know if these were meant to be rhetorical questions, but anyway I had no answers.

The others came back in time for lunch. Adam sautéed some field mushrooms with red peppers and shallots. I cooked up a pot of fettucini and served it with minced garlic in olive oil and grated Romano cheese. Arnold filled our glasses with Gevrey-Chambertin, another special treat from Dijon. J.K. made herself a tofu milkshake.

"I'll be sorry to leave," said J.K. "The pond will die."

"Dear girl," smiled Adam, "I shall care for it like my own."

Rachel passed around some sketches and paintings she'd done of Adam's place and environs.

"You have an eye for composition," admired Norman.

"Not to mention color, light and shade," said Adam.

"These are for your walls," said Rachel, handing him watercolors of the pond and the A-frame.

We had a couple of hours to spare, so we played a round of *Outrageous,* a game of wits where the object is to make the most unlikely sweeping statement. After discussion the others award points, zero to ten, for originality and cleverness in defending it.

Rachel started off: "The CIA has banned popsicles."

Her explanation, that flavored ice precipitates brain cancer and mass paranoia, although original enough and truly unlikely, was judged to be irrelevant; control over popsicles was simply outside the purview of the CIA. We gave her six points.

Adam was next. "Hair loss causes more suicides than unwanted pregnancies," he declared. "And that's not counting Poland."

"Can you prove it?" asked Norman.

Adam nodded. "I have all the data in a wall safe."

"Now wait a minute," said Rachel. "Do you mean that more people kill themselves than get pregnant because their hair falls out, or that unwanted pregnancies are responsible for fewer suicides than is the loss of hair?"

"I'd bet my butt on the latter," said Arnold.

"And if the former," I noted, "surely this proposition would apply overwhelmingly to women."

"Not necessarily," said Adam. "The man whose raucous seed hits the mark may not want to live with the consequences."

Arnold guffawed. "Raucous!!? Now that's personification if I ever heard it, not to mention projection. Semen have no conscious intent. They wriggle their way to an instinctually programmed goal. You might as well call them fervid as raucous."

Rachel was consulting *The American Heritage Dictionary.*

" 'Raucous,' " she read, " 'rough-sounding and harsh.' 'Fervid— impassioned, extremely hot, burning.' "

"I know that feeling," Norman said. "But whether my seed does, well . . ."

"A minor tongue-slip," defended Adam. "Regrettably my first language is not English. Perhaps I meant to say raunchy."

" 'Smutty, indecent, lecherous,' " read Rachel.

"There!" cried Arnold. "Your true colors are revealed!"

Adam held his hand up. "That is a wounding remark, and moreover not true," he said. "I will forgive it if you will kindly grant me leave to expound on my original statement."

We huddled and agreed.

"Once upon a time," said Adam, "there was a genie who was cooped up in a bottle for millennia. A young shepherd boy heard his cries and released him. He realized his mistake only when the genie towered high above and laughed down at him.

" 'I'm free! Now I shall have you for breakfast!' he gloated.

"The boy, a quick-witted Dummling—he embodied the opposites, you see—challenged the genie.

" 'I don't believe a thing of your size could fit into such a small container,' he scoffed. 'Would you be so kind as to show me?'

"Whereupon the genie shriveled himself back into the bottle.

" 'There,' he said with gusto. 'Now do you believe?'

" 'You're quite as dumb as you are big,' said the boy, putting the stopper back in."

"The shepherd boy buried the bottle in a far corner of a field, and to this day, though the entire area has been surveyed and optioned for mineral rights, it has not been found again."

We gave Adam eight points; not because we understood the story, but because maybe he did.[75]

At four o'clock we were ready to go. We lined up to say good-bye to Adam and Norman. To my utter surprise, J.K. curtsied.

"Thanks, fellas," she said, "it's been real. Well, sort of."

My child, my budding daughter.

Rachel shook hands with Norman, then bent and planted a kiss on the top of Adam's head.

"Come and see me some time. I'll show you my etchings."

Provocative lady. I was thrilled she was mine, more or less.

"Prof," said Arnold, bear-hugging Adam, "I gotta hand it to you, you sure know how to cook."

---

[75] I subsequently learned that this was Adam's version of a Grimm fairytale, itself a distillation of other folklore, and moreover that Jung had devoted several pages to its psychological interpretation in "The Spirit Mercurius" (*Alchemical Studies,* CW 13, pars. 239-246). I didn't hold this against Adam; only maybe he didn't deserve so many points.

The big lummox. He wouldn't know a taste bud from a turnip.

Sunny jumped in the air. "Arf!" she barked. "Arf! Arf!"

Vintage Sunny. She always makes a spectacle of herself when I'm about to leave, just like a little kid: "Don't forget me!"

I kneeled down and embraced Adam. He felt uncommonly frail and I had a sudden fear that he wouldn't be around for long. My eyes filled with tears and when we broke apart I could see that his had too.

"Shoo!" he said, wiping his glasses.

Rachel took off beeping, with J.K. and Arnold. I was right behind, with Sunny in the back savaging a biscuit.

Adam and the A-frame slowly receded in my rear-view mirror.

The big A? Well, maybe so, maybe no, but big enough for me.

"Drive safely," he called, "and come back decent."

Deo concedente.

Bibliography

Carus, Carl Gustav. *Psyche*. Zürich: Spring Publications, 1970.

Clark, Ella Elizabeth. *Indian Legends of Canada*. Toronto: McClelland and Stewart, 1960.

Daumal, René. *Mount Analogue*. Trans. Roger Shattuck. London: Vincent Stuart Ltd., 1959.

Edinger, Edward F. *The Creation of Consciousness: Jung's Myth for Modern Man*. Toronto: Inner City Books, 1984.

_____. *Transformation of the God-Image: An Elucidation of Jung's* Answer to Job. Toronto: Inner City Books, 1992.

_____. *The Mystery of the Coniunctio: Alchemical Image of Individuation*. Toronto: Inner City Books, 1994.

Ellenberger, Henri F. *The Discovery of the Unconscious: The History and Evolution of Dynamic Psychiatry*. New York: Basic Books, 1970.

Henri, Robert. *The Art Spirit*. New York: Harper and Row, 1984.

Jaffé, Aniela, ed. *C.G. Jung: Word and Image* (Bollingen Series XCVII.2). Princeton: Princeton University Press, 1979.

Johnston, Basil. *Ojibway Heritage: Ceremonies, Rituals and Legends of the Ojibway*. Toronto: McClelland and Stewart, 1976.

Jung, C.G. *The Collected Works* (Bollingen Series XX). 20 vols. Trans. R.F.C. Hull. Ed. H. Read, M. Fordham, G. Adler, Wm. McGuire. Princeton: Princeton University Press, 1953-1979.

Norman, Marsha. *The Fortune Teller*. New York: Bantam Books, 1988.

Pearen, Shelley J. *Exploring Manitoulin*. Toronto: University of Toronto Press, 1992.

Sharp, Daryl. *The Secret Raven: Conflict and Transformation*. Toronto: Inner City Books, 1980.

_____. *Personality Types: Jung's Model of Typology*. Toronto: Inner City Books, 1987.

_____. *The Survival Papers: Anatomy of a Midlife Crisis*. Toronto: Inner City Books, 1988.

_____. *Dear Gladys: The Survival Papers, Book 2*. Toronto: Inner City Books, 1989.

_____. *Jung Lexicon: A Primer of Terms and Concepts.* Toronto: Inner City Books, 1991.

_____. *Getting To Know You: The Inside Out of Relationship.* Toronto: Inner City Books, 1992.

_____. *Chicken Little: The Inside Story (A Jungian Romance).* Toronto: Inner City Books, 1993.

von Franz, Marie-Louise. *On Divination and Synchronicity: The Psychology of Meaningful Chance.* Toronto: Inner City Books, 1980.

Index

Jung, C.G. *(cont.):*
  Mysterium Coniunctionis, 46
  "On the Nature of the Psyche," 47
  "On the Psychology of the Uncon-
    scious," 38
  Psychology and Alchemy, 46, 61, 116
  Psychology and Religion, 118
  "Psychology of the Child Archetype,
    The," 81-83
  "Psychology of the Transference,"
    The," 46
  "Relations Between the Ego and the
    Unconscious, The," 38-39, 60
  "Spirit Mercurius, The," 136n
  "Syzygy: Anima and Animus, The,"
    112
  "Technique of Differentiation, The,"
    103
  *Two Essays on Analytical
    Psychology,* 38-39, 60, 118-120
Jung, Emma, 99

Kafka, Franz, 46, 129
Klein, Melanie, 54
knee, as seat of soul, 113
Kohut, Hans, 54

Letters to a Young Poet, 16
liver, as seat of soul, 61
Logos, 98, 125
love, versus force, 124

magical thinking, 30
magician, 111, 114
mana, 87, 96, 99
mana-personality, 87-88, 95-96, 109-
  121
Manitou, 12, 25, 107
Manitoulin: 12-14, 40, 87-88, 105-108
  maps, 13, 106
Mesmer, Franz Anton, 36n
metaphor, 31, 44-45, 49, 119, 128, 132
moods, 92-95, 98, 109-110
morality, 39, 120-121, 132-134
mother complex, 17, 88, 93-95, 114

Mount Analogue, 113n
multiple personalities, 23-24, 28, 30-31,
  60
Mystery of the Coniunctio, The, 95n
myth/mythology, 24, 31-32, 42, 50,
  125, 133

Nanabozho, 50, 107
necessity, 48
neurosis, 28-29, 81-82, 113, 127-131
New Age, 55-57, 119
Niederdorf, 11, 62, 131
Nietzsche, Friedrich, 118
Norman, 21, 30, 42-43, 46-49, 55, 63-
  64, 68-69, 78-80, 84, 87, 89-94,
  96-100, 103-104, 107-117, 122,
  134-137
Norman, Marsha, 64n
numinous/numinosity, 23, 84

objective psyche, 27, 67, 69, 123, 134
Ojibway, 12, 16, 50
On Divination and Synchronicity, 72n
opinions, 43, 98-101, 109-110
opposites, 10, 20, 72, 84, 95, 114-116,
  123, 129-130, 132, 136
Outrageous, 134-136

parents, 26-27, 31, 33, 40-41, 73-75, 79-80,
  88, 117
participation mystique, 55-56, 79-80
Pearen, Shelley J., 108
perfection, 132
Perseus, 31
persona, 27, 33-36, 38, 46-48, 50, 65-
  66, 76, 83, 90-94
personality: 7, 23, 25-30, 33-36, 40-50,
  52, 54, 66-70, 75-76, 85, 122-134
  of analyst, 126-127
  redeemer, 58-60
Personality Types, 78n
Philosophers' Stone, 116
Pierce, David M., 16
pond, 52, 54-55, 64, 68-69, 71, 73
possession, 28-29, 49, 92, 101, 111

Studies in Jungian Psychology
by Jungian Analysts

Quality Paperbacks